The
PRACTICES
of a
HEALTHY CHURCH

The
PRACTICES
of a
HEALTHY CHURCH

*Biblical Strategies
for Vibrant Church Life
and Ministry*

Donald J. MacNair
with Esther L. Meek

P&R
P U B L I S H I N G
P.O. BOX 817 • PHILLIPSBURG • NEW JERSEY 08865-0817

Unless otherwise indicated, all Scripture quotations are from the HOLY BIBLE, NEW INTERNATIONAL VERSION®. NIV®. Copyright © 1973, 1978, 1984 by International Bible Society. Used by permission of Zondervan Publishing House. All rights reserved. Italics indicate emphasis added.

Page design by Tobias Design
Typesetting by Michelle Feaster

Printed in the United States of America

Library of Congress Cataloging-in-Publication Data

MacNair, Donald J., 1922–
    The practices of a healthy church : biblical strategies for vibrant
church life and ministry / Donald J. MacNair ; with Esther L. Meek.
        p.   cm.
    ISBN 0-87552-390-0 (pbk.)
    1. Church growth.   I. Meek, Esther L., 1953–.   II. Title.
BV652.25.M319 1999
254'.5—dc21   99-26138

*To the elders of many churches
who have inspired my thought and practice.*
—*D. J. M.*

*To my mother, my husband, and others
who have enabled me to write.*
—*E. L. M.*

Contents

Contents

Foreword

I should have used better judgment.

My father was visiting my family in St. Louis, and so I invited him to come with me to the local church where I was the guest preacher.

My father's and my church roots are in the rural South. I grew up listening to him, a layman, preach in little churches with peeling paint, where cows grazed beyond the windows and blackberries grew in the briars just beyond the gravel where our cars were parked. During the summer, we kept the air moving across our faces with cardboard fans from the local funeral home; during the winter, we tried to find seats in the sanctuary that were just the right distance from the coal stove to keep from burning (if we were too close) or freezing (if we were too far away). We sang without accompaniment, and afterwards ate without restraint from the covered dish dinners that were majestically laid out on the available tables.

When I was in seventh grade, my father's company transferred him to St. Louis. We began worshiping in middle-class, suburban churches. But after five years, my father's discomfort moved him back to our Southern home, where he could resume worshiping in the setting that he knew and in the style that he believed to be most true to Scripture. College, seminary, and then pastoral obligations of my own kept me from many more opportunities to worship with him in those rural settings that I knew from childhood; over the years, the memory of my roots dimmed.

But I remembered my youth with rising panic as he and I drove into the parking lot of the big city church whose sign out front advertised "Contemporary Worship." Worshipers poured out of Chevy Blazers and Chrysler vans wearing denim shirts and casual pants. Teenagers of both genders had earrings in at least one ear.

Guiding my father to a molded plastic chair as the lead guitarist in the praise band hit a lick from a rock version of "Rock of Ages," I knew that we were in trouble. I tried to reassure my father that everything would be okay once the time came for me to preach. But I could not really hide from him or myself how ill prepared we both were for this experience.

I watched my father trying not to be noticed for his non-participation in the music and praise that made the young people around us sway and raise their hands. He tried to look respectful, but he really looked lost and small in what was to him an alien worship setting. I was not the only one to sense his discomfort.

After the service, a man who thirty years earlier had befriended my father during his St. Louis sojourn came over to greet him. "Wayman," said the friend, "I know how uncomfortable this music makes you feel. I don't like it either."

Then, with an expansive wave of his hand that in my mind's eye must have been something like the gesture Jesus made when He told His disciples to look at the fields ripe for harvest, the man continued: "But look at all the young people who come to hear about the Savior. I have stayed with this church all these years, because God is using it even in ways I can't always appreciate."

That man was Don MacNair. The words he spoke to my father disclose much of the essence of the man. Throughout his ministry, Don has committed himself to the work of the church and the expansion of her ministry, sacrificing his own interests in order that the truth of God's Word and the love of the Savior might spread unhindered.

Don originally trained to be an engineer, but then God called him to prepare for pastoral ministry. Precision indeed shows in his thought and writing, but no stereotype of a near-sighted, narrow-minded man will fit him. His passion for Christ and the church has always drawn him beyond the caricatures to fresh possibilities.

Among his several pastorates, Don ministered in a church once pastored by Francis Schaeffer. By the time of Don's ministry, that church needed the vision, will, and energy to move from a restricted setting to a place where it could engage the new potential that God was bringing to its membership. Overcoming objections about tampering with historic traditions, Don brought the will and the energy for the requisite change.

That church produced leaders who formed the backbone of a new denomination of conservative Presbyterians committed to the truth of God's Word. In his broom-closet-turned-office in that church building, a group of men—led by Don—prayerfully committed themselves to draw up plans for a seminary that could one day train students from around the world, equipping them for ministry around the world. A little of the engineer in Don showed then: he helped survey the property on which the seminary would take shape. But more important was his leadership in this strategic kingdom venture.

Don left that church to head his denomination's agency to start new churches. In that post, he not only gave visionary leadership to the denomination's mission efforts, but also worked with interdenominational agencies to multiply churches and the work of the gospel.

When his small denomination began to consider merging with a larger one with similar confessional commitments, Don became one of the chief proponents of the cause, though he knew that the union would ultimately deprive him of his position.

When that happened, Don formed a small consulting company, dedicating his extensive church experience and insight to helping churches revitalize their ministries—a lively ministry he continues to this day.

Whether acting as a pastor, a denominational officer, an author, a teacher, or a consultant, Don MacNair has made himself a servant of Christ's church. His vast experience has made him an expert who could now choose simply to dispense the wisdom he has gained. Instead, Don is always thinking ahead, always considering what new challenges the present age presents for the church, and always seeking to discover more specifically how the Bible (rather than tradition, comfortable habits, or past practices) should guide us in expanding and improving the ministry of the local church.

This latest of Don's books, coming near the end of his earthly ministry, is one of his most innovative. He refuses to be locked into traditional structures in considering how a church's leaders and people can combine their gifts to gain a vision of what God would have them do. It is my guess that Don found it personally uncomfortable to say some of the things he felt he needed to say in this book. Much as when he spoke to my father in the contemporary church setting, I hear Don saying, "Personally, I would be a whole lot more comfortable with more traditional ways. But I am driven by the priorities of my Savior."

Just before I was married, I sought Don's advice on how to handle all the budgeting, insurance, and mortgage concerns that now loomed so large before me. It was probably presumptuous for a young seminarian to walk into the office of a national church leader and ask such a question. But I had spent lots of time with Don's children in his home during my high school years, and I knew that he would care about my concerns. He did. He advised me on what to do; he also encouraged me not to worry about not having all the answers right away—as long as I kept taking my concerns to the Lord.

At that time, Don MacNair prepared me for my bride. He has given his life to preparing the church to be an ever more glorious bride for Christ. In this book, Don MacNair continues that ministry, not by claiming to have the final answer, but by telling us to make sure that we keep dealing with our church concerns in the way that our Lord directs.

Bryan Chapell
President of Covenant Theological Seminary

Chapter 1 Church Health: What It Is, Why It's Important, How to Get It

Church Growth and Church Health

Many books have been published on church growth. With your mind's eye, you can picture a bookstore shelf so labeled, filled with such books. If I could, I would like to designate a spot on the shelf just to the right, labeled "Church Health." Perhaps this book you are holding today is one of only a few shelved there (more likely, you will have found this book in the "Church Growth" section!). But in the years to come, it would be best for books on church health to proliferate.

Right away let me assert that my championing of church health does not mean that I oppose church growth! We cannot take these two to be in conflict, by any means. The issue is, rather, one of focus.

In our American preoccupation with success, church growth is easily identified with increasing numbers of people sitting in the pews and participating in the programs. It would be a struggle to think otherwise!

But how can a Christian knock numerical growth? Presumably it indicates that people are turning to Christ, and certainly that is what churches want to see!

The sad reality, however, is that a church that focuses merely on numbers most likely will become an unhealthy church. When numbers rule, an organization feels justified in resorting to any means to increase them. This attitude prevails in many businesses, and employees have found their own job satisfaction decrease significantly. The comic strip *Dilbert* poignantly expresses this malaise.

A similar scenario can occur in a church. In fact, churches can feel pressured to "produce" in order to continue "selling their product," in accordance with the prevailing societal mind-set. The problem for employees is that the overweening commitment to the bottom line discounts practically every other factor that makes for healthy, happy work experiences. The problem for churches is essentially the same, with the terms adjusted, and, unfortunately, with the stakes much higher. When a church is primarily committed to numerical growth, it easily accepts the lowest possible standards of commitment and a lifestyle that conforms to the world's practices. The pursuit of spiritual maturity falls by the wayside.

If church growth is defined as an increase in the number of involved people, then church must be about much more than growth. In fairness, many people who discuss church growth declare that it means more than just increasing numbers. Yet the unhealthy focus persists. The problem may lie with our American mentality: it's very difficult for us to avoid reducing the word *growth* to the word *numbers*. Pastors, elders, and members deeply involved with their local congregations, when talking shop with people similarly committed to other congregations, cannot resist the temptation to say something like: "Our church is growing; God is blessing us; our attendance is now up over 300!" Or people will (reluctantly) say: "Our attendance is falling off; we're not growing; God is not blessing."

For this and other reasons, I believe that the church should focus on health rather than growth. I am writing to persuade you to think in terms of health. I hope to show you the difference it will make as your congregation thinks this way, and I want to show you the how-tos of a healthy church.

You'll soon find that a healthy church *will grow*. But growth must always be defined in terms of the maturing image of Christ in individual members as well as in the church body as a whole. You will also find that the growth of a healthy church will be *natural*, rather than artificially contrived. It will happen as the Holy Spirit works sovereignly—"as God causes it to grow" (Col. 2:19).

God's Agenda Too!

The word *health* also more aptly expresses God's own intention for the church. Using the metaphor of a bridegroom (Christ) and His bride (the church), the apostle Paul tells us: "Christ loved the church and gave himself up for her to make her holy, cleansing her by the washing with water through the word, and to present her to himself as a radiant church, without stain or wrinkle or any other blemish, but holy and blameless" (Eph. 5:25–27). The church's goal is to "grow up into him who is the Head, that is, Christ," says Paul elsewhere in the same letter, now using the metaphor of the head (Christ) and the body (the church) (Eph. 4:15). He also tells us that we were "predestined to be conformed to the likeness of his Son," and that to this end "in all things God works for the good of those who love him" (Rom. 8:28–29). Thus, "we proclaim him, admonishing and teaching everyone with all wisdom, so that we may present everyone perfect in Christ. To this end I labor, struggling with all his energy, which so powerfully works in me" (Col. 1:28–29).

These verses describe growth that is best defined as motion toward spiritual maturity, or Christlikeness. Individuals must be growing: believers must be moving toward spiritual maturity, and unbelievers (future believers!) must evidence movement toward embracing Christ. The body must also be growing: the church as a whole must conform more and more to the beautiful biblical metaphors of the bride and the body, and must also be extending to include new believers. To focus on this motion toward Christlikeness is to focus on health. What is more, it is both to obey God and to share His very own agenda. It is reasonable and right to expect that a church that adopts God's agenda of health, and that strives to take seriously His own pattern for the church, will receive His blessing. It only makes sense to think that God will deem the biblically conformed church to be His most effective instrument to spread His kingdom.

A Church It's Wonderful to Be a Part Of!

Focusing on health is not only important and obedient; it's also beneficial! To focus on health is to focus on what is truly good, on what God Himself intended, for both individual believers and local bodies. To focus on health is to long for that motion toward godliness that characterizes both the believer and the seeker, and that characterizes both small and large churches. Individual spiritual growth is given primacy, because corporate growth, both quantitative and qualitative, springs from its soil. Outreach that focuses on health refuses to be satisfied with the mere presence of another physical body within the church doors (I exaggerate to point out the distinction!), but seeks to disciple, to teach Christ, to make righteousness attractive, at whatever point it finds the unbeliever. It leaves the outcomes to the Holy Spirit, while eagerly anticipating His working.

Imagine the changes that might occur in a workplace that consciously shifted its focus from the bottom line to customer service and employee satisfaction! Wouldn't that office become a noticeably better place to work? Perhaps profits would increase less rapidly at the outset, but in the end profits might even increase more rapidly, because of happy, productive workers, customers who find they can rely on quality, and an increasingly good name for the company. It's just as easy to imagine what a change in focus would mean for a church that has been driven by numbers. A church with members who are growing in the Lord and who have together come to anticipate joyfully God's further blessing is just about the most attractive church you can imagine; it's the one that will grow, and grow naturally.

On the other side, many churches have neither been driven by numbers nor done anything but maintain the status quo for years. For these churches, the biblical summons to health may come as an unwanted reveille. It may feel uncomfortable at first to begin to move toward health. No (self-initiated) change for the better can occur without dissatisfaction with the status quo, without the honesty to admit the need for change, without the courage to seek a better arrangement, and without the determination to accomplish it. All of these things require a tough-mindedness that rarely comes naturally—and that we initially resist! "Oh, how I hate to get up in the morning!"—no World War II veteran will forget Irving Berlin's words!

But everybody who has ever experienced both the status quo (out of shape!) and good health would concur that the struggle was worth it, for health really feels much better. "No pain, no gain," we say; it's true of everything from organizing a closet to building a skyscraper, from physical health to church health.

The Analogy of Physical Health

Biblical church health is important, obedient, and beneficial. As I have indicated, the concept of health more aptly expresses our proper goal than does the concept of growth. I intend to devote this entire book to communicating the concept of church health.

We must begin by specifying what we mean by "health." We can do this most easily by talking about physical health, and then drawing the analogy of a healthy church body. Also, I will then be able to express more concretely some of my claims about church health.

Physical health has several aspects, and we can use the word *healthy* to describe any one of them. Perhaps most basically, we identify health with what we call wellness. Wellness is an intangible quality, a feeling of well-being that is more than physical; it is what we treasure and pursue and count ourselves blessed if we have—"We're fortunate to have our health," we say. This is what doctors and hospitals nowadays present themselves as producing, but we know that neither they nor anything short of God Himself can guarantee wellness to anyone.

Wellness has its measurable aspects. We have the energy we need; we don't catch colds very often; we have a good complexion; our clothes fit comfortably! Health is not simply an intangible; in fact, it would be hard to conceive of having the intangible in the absence of the concrete, and vice versa.

The fact that God alone can guarantee wellness doesn't in the least mean that we can or ought to do nothing! One thing that doctors do is to look for *evidences* of health. They always take our pulse, our temperature, and our blood pressure. They talk of "vital signs," data that indicate that we are healthy. The signs give the doctor basic information about our physical condition.

Then there are the things that we need to do in order to stay healthy. Eating a healthy diet, exercising regularly, getting enough sleep, avoiding stress—we need to carry out these *practices* if we wish to maintain or improve wellness. And although these practices do not guarantee wellness, we reasonably conclude that a person who does them is a healthy person. In fact, because these practices represent the steps we can actively take in pursuit of health, we are justified in concentrating most of our attention on doing them better. And I probably don't need to add that being faithful in these practices takes a great deal of perseverance!

Extending the picture further, we can say that physical health also involves some kind of standard or manual. Perhaps you want to look like a fashion model, or you want to have the strength of a certain athlete. Perhaps your doctor or hospital is sending you pamphlets to educate you concerning wellness and how to achieve it. Perhaps you've consulted a dietitian and received a specific diet plan. Perhaps your aerobics instructor stipulates a certain routine. All of these give us a sense of the goal and how to achieve it.

One last aspect: often there is a doctor, a nutritionist, or an exercise instructor—another human agent you employ to assess your health and guide and motivate you in improving it.

Wellness

You rightly surmise that every one of these aspects of physical health corresponds to something in the church body discussed in this book! Yes, ultimately the health of a local church lies in the hands of our sovereign Lord, as do all outcomes. It's very, very important to realize this! It reminds us of our utter dependence on Him; it causes us to worship Him alone; it keeps us on our knees in prayer. It preserves a balanced perspective to remember that the church is both an organism and an organization. *Organization* refers to the concrete structures, procedures, rules of operation, and plans that make up a local church—the programs you can read about in the bulletin. It would be a grave mistake to identify the church with the organization, overlooking the essential intangible aspect without which it is not a church. The "organism" of the church is its life and ministry, God's intangible working among the people, causing them to grow—and grow together. The organism is the living body or bride of Christ.

But, on the other hand, neither is the church an organism without an organization. We do not look for church health in the absence of concrete activities in which we can engage. This is because, Scripture teaches, the sovereign Lord is the covenant Lord. In relating to His people, both in redemption and in creation, God sovereignly chooses how He will act, and then He binds Himself to act that way faithfully. Having redeemed His people, choosing them not on the basis of their performance, but out of His own unconditional love, He calls them to obey His law. If we obey, we can expect His blessing; if we disobey, we can expect His judgment. In both blessing and judgment, He remains utterly faithful to His own word.

In creation it is essentially the same. God sovereignly chooses to place us in a world in which, for example, a combination of sunlight, nutrients, and water makes a plant grow. If we deny a plant one of those ingredients, it won't grow; if we give it these three according to its needs, we can reasonably expect it to grow. And we can expect that this relationship will hold tomorrow, next year, and next century, because God binds Himself to His own stipulation. To expect this with confidence is to trust His faithfulness.

The same dynamic holds with physical health and with church health. We can't guarantee wellness ultimately, but God Himself calls us to faithful pursuit of His plan, expecting His blessing, which is just what we mean by trust. We cannot guarantee the ultimate outcome, but there is much that He intends for us to do. We organize; in faith, we expect organic life. We minister; in faith we anticipate growth. We do healthy things in confident pursuit of healthy results.

Healthy results are intangible things like organism and life and God's blessing. Healthy results also include concrete things like, yes, numbers!—more members, more conversions, more kids at Bible school. But the cheerful survival of a building program also counts as a concrete result. So do members talking to their neighbors about Christ or faithfully pursuing righteousness in the workplace, or showing mercy in the community, or running godly, orderly households.

Vital Signs

In my ministry as a church consultant, I rely regularly on two evidences of a church's health. These correspond to a human body's vital signs. A church is healthy, I can see, if two things are regularly going on: first, individual members are growing in spiritual maturity; and second, the church is actively seeking to help unbelievers come to Christ, with the confident anticipation that God will bring this about. I also look for a third evidence: the absence of any major divisions or strife in the church.

Healthy Practices

The most important thing that I wish to communicate to you is that, just as there are healthy practices for the human body, so there are certain practices in which a church must engage if it is to be healthy. These are the things we can actively strive to carry out, the ways we can actively improve our church's health. If we carry them out, we can confidently anticipate God's working in us and through us, and we'll see the covenant Lord faithfully respond, in keeping with His word. Just as we might say that a person who eats right, sleeps right, and exercises right is healthy, it is reasonable to say that a church engaged in healthy practices is a healthy church. I have come to call these practices characteristics or criteria of a healthy church. I do not mean to imply that they guarantee health. I do not mean to confuse them with that intangible wellness that is God's alone to give. I mean to say that this is what we need to be practicing in order to be healthy, and that, thanks to God's covenant faithfulness, we can confidently expect His work in us and through us. I emphasize them the way we ought to emphasize diet, sleep, and exercise: they are the healthy things we can do.

What are these healthy practices? There are six. As I list them, I will indicate the chapters in this book that develop them.

#1. The church must retain its commitment to the Holy Scriptures without compromise (chapter 3).

#2. The church must engage in regular, vibrant worship to God as the ultimate motivation for personal and corporate growth (chapter 4).

#3. The church must continually train and implement shepherd leadership (chapters 6 and 7).

#4. The church must have a mechanism for utilizing gifted member initiative with ordained elder accountability; I propose ministry centers (chapters 5 and 8).

#5. The church must have a continually modified vision and plan, unique to that church body at that time and in that community, which focuses and implements its purpose and mission (chapters 9 and 10).

#6. The church must prayerfully seek the grace of God to build commitment to biblical health (chapter 11).

God would have us be "process oriented," rather than "product oriented." That's why we need to talk more about health and less about outcomes. That's why, in this analogy, the most important aspect—the one that tells us what to do, and the one that structures this book—is the practice of health. Most often when I speak of church health, I mean the practice of health. And when I assess a particular church's health, what I look for first and foremost is whether it follows these practices. At any particular point, a church may not be seeing regular conversions and the addition of members, or perhaps certain circumstances may be making things difficult for the church. But in difficult times as well as in delightful times, God calls us to faithful obedience. He's more concerned about how we live than about what we produce. Yes, in God's time and covenant faithfulness, He does grant wellness. But our part is the process; His is the product.

The Model and the Manual

God has furnished us with both a model and a manual. Christ is the model. We've already noted that God wants to conform us to the image of His Son, that leaders strive to present us perfect in Christ, and that the church is to grow up into Him who is the Head. To look at Christ is to look at perfect spiritual health, and this is something that both the individual Christian and the Christian church as a body emulate. Why else would we call ourselves Christian, if we did not strive to emulate Christ?

Our manual is God's Word, the Holy Bible. Although you and your church believe the Bible to be the Word of God, and study and revere it accordingly, you might be surprised to learn that it affords a blueprint for a healthy church. I mean to show you that the pattern that I think yields a healthy church is the pattern that comes from the Bible. I did not concoct it; I derived it by studying Scripture and continually trying to apply what I learned to many situations. That is why I believe that to pursue health is to obey God.

Let me mention four biblical directives for church health:

1. The church must apply its universal purpose and mission to the concrete situation in which God has placed it.
2. The church must treat individual members' spiritual gifts with integrity.
3. The church's elders must lead with a view to giving an account to God.
4. The church must have elders who conform to the biblical model of shepherd leaders.

Even if I did not spell out these precepts any further, you could see that they are integrally related to the healthy practices specified in the previous section. And indeed they should be, for the Word of God stipulates or entails these practices.

A Nutritionist at Your Disposal!

Finally, my role could be compared to that of a doctor or nutritionist. I love church health because I love the church passionately. I love the church because I love Christ. As I have loved Him and His bride through years of service, He has drawn me into this ministry as a natural consequence of that service. I do what I can to educate people about church health, and I do what I can to effect it. That is precisely what I am doing as I write this book.

All of this may sound rather abstract at this point, like the well-intentioned plans of an armchair strategist. I hope that as you read further, you will see that my ideas grow directly out of my experience. I have pastored three churches, for a total of eighteen years. I have held these pastorates in an inner city, in a small town, and in an affluent suburb. I have led my denomination's church-planting outreach for another nineteen years, interacting over that period with hundreds of different church plants. I have developed a ministry of consultation, through which, during the last fourteen years, I have worked with over seventy different churches, involving over 12,000 members and friends. Plus, I help to train pastors, and many of them return to discuss matters with me.

I can tell you confidently, on the basis of this experience, that a church that employs these practices exhibits these indicators, and that God does work in and through that church. Churches that don't employ these practices do not exhibit these indicators to that extent, and do not appear to be bodies in and through which God is working significantly. The first kind of church experiences health, and the second kind is relatively unhealthy.

I write to convince you of the importance of the concept of biblical church health. I want to make you and your church long for it, to excite you to pursue it. I want to give you the strategies you'll need for the process. I want to assure you of the wonderful results that should follow. I pray earnestly that

God will use this book to accomplish His will for you and your church.

How Healthy Is Our Church?

It might seem that a book on church health would be intended for, and useful to, only unhealthy churches. But wait! Who needs to eat right, sleep right, and exercise regularly? Everybody does! The sorry reality is that we often "close the barn door after the horse has gotten out," taking these habits seriously only after our health has been broken in some measure by neglecting them. But this does not change the fact that every person, to be healthy, must employ healthy practices. You need them to recover your health; you need them to improve your health; you need them to maintain your health.

That must also be said about healthy church practices. This book is for unhealthy churches; it is also for healthy churches. You need to follow the same practices, whether you need to restore your church's health or keep it healthy. I'm not recommending that you do these things until you're healthy, and then quit. I'm recommending that they become your habitual practices from now till Christ returns.

There is one group of churches that will not be helped by the practices discussed in this book. Those are the churches that don't think they need any help. They don't recognize their own inadequacy, or they don't care about the goal. Sadly, I have found many churches that fit this description.

But the positive side of this fact is heartening: to recognize that you need to grow in health and that you can use help in doing it is to have taken the first, critical, big step toward it. As I assess a church's health, I look to see if the people in that

The **Practices** *of a* **Healthy Church**

church are willing to be helped. Obviously, what I say can't be of much use if they're not really willing to listen.

But now, assuming that you are willing to examine yourself honestly, you can begin to assess your own church's health by considering these questions. You can ponder them privately, and you can discuss them with others in the church. (These questions are also listed at the end of the chapter as questions for discussion.) Are we open to change in order better to conform to God's will for us as a church? Are many of our members evidencing spiritual growth? Do we as a congregation eagerly anticipate God's blessing on our church, including His adding to our numbers? Do members sense that their elders both care for and lead them? Do members sense that their own spiritual gifts are engaged and deemed worthwhile? Is the importance we attach to Scripture evident in all our meetings and ministries? In our corporate worship, do we sense the presence and power of the living God? How is the community different because of our church's presence in it? Have we specified a vision and plans to achieve it that realistically reflect our gifts and situation? Are disagreements within our church relatively minor?

As you discuss these things, remember another fact of life: perception is often reality. How your community perceives your church significantly determines how effective you will be able to be within it. How the congregation perceives the elders' ministry, for all intents and purposes, is what determines the authority structure of your church. How each member perceives his or her own value in the body directly affects his or her involvement. That's why you'll find, in answering these questions and digesting the substance of this book, that you'll need to listen to people, not just examine your church's plans as they've been written out in the past.

Be encouraged! The living God has your church's health as His personal agenda! He already has invested a great deal in it. He makes available both His Word and His resurrection power. And to participate in this endeavor is to share His mission and to carry it out with His fullest blessing! It's time to get down to business!

Questions for Discussion

Assess your church's health, using these questions from the text:

1. Are we open to change in order better to conform to God's will for us as a church?
2. Are many of our members evidencing spiritual growth?
3. Do we as a congregation eagerly anticipate God's blessing on our church, including His adding to our numbers?
4. Do members sense that their elders both care for and lead them?
5. Do members sense that their own spiritual gifts are engaged and deemed worthwhile?
6. Is the importance we attach to Scripture evident in all our meetings and ministries?
7. In our corporate worship, do we sense the presence and power of the living God?
8. How is the community different because of our church's presence in it?
9. Have we specified a vision and plans to achieve it that realistically reflect our gifts and situation?
10. Are disagreements within our church relatively minor?

Part I

Body Basics

Chapter 2 The Wonderful Church: God's Presence on Earth

It's important at the outset not only to define what we mean by *health* in a church context, but also to define what we mean by *church*. To state the obvious: only a body can be healthy. Only a church can exhibit church health. So before we explore further God's blueprint for church health, let's examine God's concept of a church, as well as its purpose and mission. Also, for me to communicate effectively to you about biblical church health, I need to specify a few key functions and facets of the church. Finally, I must summon you to prayer as you seek to implement God's will for your church's health.

Defining the Church: What It Is and What It Ought to Be

Definitions need not be merely clinical matters. A definition states the way a word is used. The interesting thing is that a definition often also provides the standard we're shooting for, as well as the impetus to pursue it. For example, we can define a fruit tree as a plant whose flowers eventually develop an edible portion—a clinical and unengaging definition! But this definition also suggests a standard and a motivation. Already we know what a good fruit tree is: one that produces delicious fruit in great quantities. Plus, thinking of great tasting fruit and perhaps a reputation staked on obtaining such fruit motivates me to plant a healthy tree and to nurture it as well as I can.

Defining *church* works the same way. The Bible tells us what a church is and, in the process, it tells us what a church should strive to be and inspires us to strive. In fact, knowing what the church is and is becoming fuels our pursuit of church health more than just about anything else will.

I have spent the bulk of my productive years helping churches with problems, thinking and teaching about running a church and improving its health. Stated baldly like this, my job hardly seems attractive. Why would anybody want to do that?

I realize, on reflection, that I do it simply because I love the church. And when I say "the church," I mean that spiritual organism which Scripture describes as the bride or the body of Christ. I don't identify "the church" with the problems, the organization, or even the healthy traits I discuss in this book. I identify it with the majestic reality the Bible represents. The Bible tells us what the church is, and in so doing it tells us what it is becoming. I long for that vision to be more fully realized. As you can rightly guess, I believe that to pursue it is to pursue health.

Knowing what God means the church to be drives us to actualize it. Thinking about the church provokes us to pursue church health. That is why we must begin by defining *church*.

The Bible's Vision of the Church

Hear God's Word regarding the church:

> And God placed all things under [Christ's] feet and appointed him to be head over everything for the church,

which is *his body, the fullness of him* who fills everything in every way. (Eph. 1:22–23)

Consequently, you are no longer foreigners and aliens, but fellow citizens with God's people and members of *God's household,* built on the foundation of the apostles and prophets, with Christ Jesus himself as the chief cornerstone. In him the whole building is joined together and rises to become *a holy temple* in the Lord. And in him you too are being built together to become *a dwelling in which God lives* by his Spirit. (Eph. 2:19–22; cf. 1 Tim. 3:14–15; 1 Cor. 3:16)

It was he who gave some to be apostles, some to be prophets, some to be evangelists, and some to be pastors and teachers, to prepare God's people for works of service, so that *the body of Christ* may be built up until we all reach unity in the faith and in the knowledge of the Son of God and become mature, attaining to the whole measure of the fullness of Christ. . . . [W]e will in all things grow up into him who is the Head, that is, Christ. From him *the whole body,* joined and held together by every supporting ligament, grows and builds itself up in love, as each part does its work. (Eph. 4:11–16; cf. 1 Cor. 12, especially v. 27)

For the husband is the head of the wife as Christ is the head of the church, *his body,* of which he is the Savior. . . . Husbands, love your wives, just as Christ loved the church and gave himself up for her to make her holy, cleansing her by the washing with water through the word, and to present her to himself as a radiant church, without stain or wrinkle or any other blemish, but holy and blameless. . . . [N]o one ever hated his own body, but he feeds and cares for it, just as Christ does the church—for we are members of *his body*. . . . This is a profound mystery—but I am talking about Christ and the church. (Eph. 5:23–32; cf. Rev. 19:7; 21:2, 9–10)

Is the church primarily a physical structure of bricks and wood? Is it primarily a program of weekly activities? Is it a set of problems, or even a set of plans? Is it a set of people interacting in terms of programs, problems, and plans? We can agree that the church often involves these things. But without another ingredient, all of these things taken together would fall short of being a church.

The Scripture passages quoted above imply that the church is primarily a spiritual organism with a mystical relationship to God. When I say that it is "spiritual," I do not mean "unreal"! I do mean "nonphysical." In the Old Testament, the temple in Jerusalem and the portable tabernacle prior to it constituted a geographical locus of God's presence. The New Testament says that believers together now constitute God's temple, His dwelling. It talks of believers as living stones being built together into a spiritual house. This is a spiritual reality, not a physical one. Yes, we have church buildings; we meet in "sanctuaries." But what sets them apart is that God dwells in the believers who gather there. Were they to assemble in a gym or a ballroom, that place would be special because they are.

I speak of the church as an "organism." The church is not merely a group of people. It is a living entity of its own. God the Holy Spirit indwells and enlivens individual believers. But these verses and others indicate clearly that the Holy Spirit indwells and enlivens believers as a group that we call the church. We don't just get together because we have some things in common; together we *are* a single thing, a living organism. We are not individuals or even individuals who get along; we are body parts, living stones—parts of a single, living whole. God Himself takes individual believers and does more than just group them; He knits them together into a new living entity. He breaks down walls that divide us, making us one in Christ.

What the Bible says about this living organism is nothing short of amazing! The spiritual organism has a special, mystical relationship with the living God. The church does not simply express solidarity with Christ's claims, seeking converts to a cause. The church does not simply consist of people who have let Christ's sacrifice substitute for their own. God calls this spiritual organism *His household* and *His temple* in which He dwells on earth. He calls the church *the bride of Christ.* A bride forms a special union with her husband. God designates the church to be *the body of Christ,* that is, the very organism that *is* Christ on earth, "the fullness of him who fills everything in every way." Each metaphor—dwelling, bride, body—drives the church and Christ closer to each other with its portrayal, so that, in the end, Scripture is describing what amounts to an identity, a mystical union.

The church is the presence of Christ on earth. Jesus, of course, was God Himself in the flesh, in time and space, by God's will and for His glory. What Ephesians is telling us is that, for the time between Christ's two advents, *the church* is God Himself, in the Spirit, in time and space, by His will and for His glory.

We get so used to the biblical phrases that we lose sight of their awesome reality. God has chosen in this age to identify Himself with His church. The church *is Christ* to the world.

The world should never be able to escape the evidence that Christ is very much here on earth in His church.

Let this reality command center stage in your thoughts! With so grand an identity at issue, how can we allow our focus to wander to petty differences and matters of personal comfort or aggrandizement? The glory of God—His presence—matters so much more.

Here we have—thinking back to the example of the fruit tree—the definition and at least part of the incentive. Obviously, we also have the standard. The definition of *church* as the presence of Christ on earth also indicates what a good church is. A good church is one which accurately represents Christ to the world, one which is a healthy spiritual organism, fully embodying this mystical union. Moving closer and closer to Christlikeness, "growing up into the Head, that is, Christ," is what the Bible says the church is supposed to be doing.

When God became human, He indwelt a body—human, but sinless. In the church, God identifies Himself with humanity again, this time with a group purchased by Christ, but still plagued by sin. Oh, the extent of His grace and love! But He does not intend to leave things as they are. Like a home buyer purchasing a "fixer-upper," God marries a bride riddled with blemishes and covered with grime, and sets about perfecting her: "Christ loved the church and gave himself up for her to make her holy, cleansing her by the washing with water through the word, and to present her to himself as a radiant church, without stain or wrinkle or any other blemish, but holy and blameless." For one thing, not all the parts are in the body yet; for another, we all need to be cleaned up. That is what the Holy Spirit is taking care of now. The book of Revelation, describing the end of time, speaks of the wedding of the Lamb, when the bride has made herself ready with the fine linen, bright and clean, given her to wear (19:7–8). She is radiant; she is perfect; she is fully God's dwelling with people (21:2–3, 9–14). That is the completed, perfected church.

How can the world see Christ in a sin-ridden collection of converts? What the world should see is Christ at work. When something changes a hardened criminal into a humble benefactor, when loving relationships grow across ethnic or racial barriers, when people keep promises and tell the truth even to their own hurt, or when a congregation mercifully addresses a community need, the world will recognize the presence of supernatural power and holiness.

My personal experience is that the glorious reality makes me long for its fruition. I earnestly hope that your experience does the same for you. For to long for its fruition is to long for your church's health. I want my church to look more like the radiant bride, to look more like Christ Himself! I want the body to grow up into its Head; I want our corporate spiritual maturity. I want more of the fullness of Christ. You or I cannot do it alone, for this is an attribute of the group, the body. The members of your church together must long for body health.

This longing must motivate us to be part of a process that will last for the rest of our lives and will continue for the entire duration of the church—till Christ returns. It must so motivate us that we as a group accept challenges that move us on from the status quo in pursuit of God's ways. It will be one challenge after another, as long as we are sinful people inhabiting a continually changing world. But "let us fix our eyes on Jesus, the author and perfecter of our faith, who for the joy set before him endured the cross, scorning its shame, and sat down at the right hand of the throne of God. Consider him who endured such opposition from sinful men, so that you will not grow weary and lose heart"—so that we may "throw off everything that hinders and the sin that so easily entangles, and . . . run with perseverance the race marked out for us" (Heb. 12:1–3).

The Purpose of the Church

The church is the presence of Christ on earth. We can rework this glorious definition of the church to express its purpose. Why does my church exist? Why does any evangelical church exist? Every church possesses the same purpose. The church exists to express the presence of God on earth.

The church also exists to lead the earth in praising and worshiping God. The picture of the bride, used by both New and Old Testaments (see Hosea 1–3), captures this feature as well. A radiant bride makes the most ordinary man look really good! Sometimes it works the other way! Also, a good spouse brings honor to his or her mate, showing respect by taking the other's affairs seriously, complying with requests willingly, and maintaining faithfulness to their covenant. A good spouse is often the other's "number one fan." Similarly, seeing the church as Christ's bride helps us realize that we exist to bring Christ glory. While the groom is busy adorning the bride, the bride is busy adoring the groom. In fact, God uses the adoring to accomplish the adorning. Thus, worship is our priority, and it also furnishes our motivation for change, as we will see in a later chapter. We are "a people belonging to God, that [we] may declare the praises of him who called [us] out of darkness into his wonderful light" (1 Peter 2:9). He's building us, His living stones, "into a spiritual house to be a holy priesthood, offering spiritual sacrifices acceptable to God through Jesus Christ" (2:5).

That is how the church leads the world in worship to its Lord. The church exists also to demonstrate the presence of

Christ to the world. Local churches need to think seriously about this glorious truth. Like a definition, it functions both as description and norm: that is what we are, and that is what we should strive to be. The idea of the presence of Christ, when practically considered, has to do with self-perception and community perception. Concretely, we need to consider seriously how we perceive ourselves and how our community perceives our church.

While each church shares the same purpose of demonstrating Christ's presence on earth, the fact that each church resides in a particular place—geographically, culturally, and historically—means that demonstrating Christ's presence will necessarily vary from church to church. You will see this as we look at concrete examples. You will see it again in later chapters as each church's unique vision gives concrete expression to the church's common purpose and mission. An idea so abstract that it does not engage a concrete situation would be pretty useless.

It's quite possible that, for all our good intentions, people in our community do not consider us to be representing Christ to them. Here are some experiences I have had that have made me ponder this. First, although it is good for a community's financial and social stability for there to be churches in the area, it is also the case that a church building, parking lot, and accompanying traffic undermine the value of houses around it. This is true no matter how beautiful your facility happens to be. A house is more difficult to sell if there is a church next door, even if it is a handsome building surrounded by well-manicured grounds.

This means that the church needs to overcome a natural perception, in order to be to the neighborhood the earthly presence of Christ. Unless we relate personally to people, our very presence will antagonize them. A pastor in a suburban church made calls in the neighborhood until he knew everyone who lived there. His church welcomed the use of its facility for public meetings. A subsequent pastor did not maintain this contact. During his tenure, when the congregation applied for permission to remodel the building, they encountered stiff opposition from the community.

The current pastor of that church has reinstated neighborhood visiting. He has talked to everyone who lives in the neighborhood, building bridges by being involved in their lives. The church once again requested permission to build. The subdivision approved the request. This suggests that the community now perceives the church more as people with conviction than as a public building.

Some churches disregard the appearance of their buildings. Of course, true spirituality must be distinguished from appearance, but when it comes to relating to the community, even demonstrating the presence of Christ to the community, appearance can be important. A run-down building says, in effect, "We don't care about our community"—not the sort of thing we can picture the Lord Jesus saying! A neat building says, "We want to do whatever we can to make our community as nice as possible."

A church on the outskirts of a major city asked me to consult with them. I purposely arrived ahead of our scheduled meeting, and I used the time to walk around the building and to talk to people in the community—probably not something the church would have asked me to do! I was trying to find out how the community perceived that church.

One thing I found was the long-dried remains of eggs thrown against the church's walls! Later, I took the elders around to see it. They hadn't even noticed it, even though they passed it regularly! The eggs projected the message that this church didn't care what the community thought. My talks with neighbors confirmed the message of the eggs.

It is simply not possible to persuade the people in the community that we represent Christ if we do not first express a heartfelt interest in and concern for them. Think of Jesus, speaking to the woman at the well, singling out Zacchaeus, eating with Matthew's friends, and calling fishermen to follow Him. Sense His personal care, a care that broke down barriers and opened hearts to His message. Of course, we can't demonstrate the presence of Christ merely by keeping our flower beds nice, but we can't demonstrate the presence of Christ if we don't.

I can think of common church mentalities that thwart any expression of Christ's presence in a community. One is what we often call a *fortress mentality*. A local church can communicate that its sole goal is to protect itself from being tainted by its evil surroundings. As a young seminary student, I interned at a church whose Sunday morning attendance averaged one hundred, but whose rolls contained only fifteen to eighteen members! To be a member at that church, you had to sign a vow each year to abstain from drinking, smoking, and movies. This communicated that would-be members had to attain certain standards in order to be good enough—a message directly contrary to the gospel of the Lord Jesus Christ. How can a church demonstrate the presence, the body, of Christ when it limits its membership more stringently than does Christ Himself, and if it does not freely offer the good news to all?

Closely related to a fortress mentality is a *maintenance mentality*. In this case, the community perceives that a church mostly wants to be left alone to preserve what it already has. One church of 2,500 members that I worked with communicated to people in the town that its members felt that they had "arrived," that they were superior citizens. How? By calling their church "First Church." They were perceived as egotists, thus undermining their testimony.

One church I served as a consultant typified a maintenance mentality. Ostensibly, they wanted to hire a youth director, thinking that an influx of young people would enable this congregation of people over sixty-five years old to maintain their existence (note the word *maintain!*). At bottom, they really wanted to stay the same, avoid change, and preserve the status quo. But they knew they were dying, and that threatened their commitment to maintenance.

Had they hired such a youth director, that person would have quickly discovered real opposition to his or her use of the facilities—the church wanted to preserve them, too! They didn't want the building worn out. Can you imagine a church not wanting to use its building? Strange as it sounds, it can be a strong temptation. You know as well as I do that a building should be used, not just on Sunday, but as much as possible. The more a church's facilities are used, the more that church can serve the Lord.

I counseled the people in that church to seek God seriously through a prayer vigil, to prepare themselves to change gears to reach out to families with children, rather than employing a youth director and tying one of his hands behind his back. In effect, I was challenging their maintenance mentality, and calling them to demonstrate the presence of Christ. I was no help to them.

But now, here are some examples of churches that have attempted to align perceptions with the reality of reflecting Christ. When one church moved from the city to the suburbs, the people took advantage of the opportunity to change its name, replacing one fraught with rigid historical distinctives and past battles with one that expressed their spiritual commitment. In so doing, they expressed that they valued commitment to Christ and to people in the here and now, distancing themselves from a focus that would have been little appreciated by the community.

That church also revised its elder preparation process. They wanted to evidence Christ by allowing newer members access to service in leadership, rather than restricting leadership to a handful of well-seasoned, long-term members. In order to do this, while maintaining the integrity of their theological position, the church instituted a lengthy period of training between the nomination and the election of officers. They communicated that in this church, everybody's important.

The Church's Mission

Every evangelical local church shares the same definition, the same purpose, and also the same mission. Who are we? We are the presence of God on earth. Why are we here? We're here to express God's presence to the world and to lead the world in worshiping Him. What are we to do?

The mission of the church is to fulfill God's will on earth. God's will for the church consists of the Great Commission, which Jesus gave shortly before He ascended to heaven:

> Then the eleven disciples went to Galilee, to the mountain where Jesus had told them to go. When they saw him, they worshiped him; but some doubted. Then Jesus came to them and said, "All authority in heaven and on earth has been given to me. Therefore go and make

disciples of all nations, baptizing them in the name of the Father and of the Son and of the Holy Spirit, and teaching them to obey everything I have commanded you. And surely I am with you always, to the very end of the age. (Matt. 28:16–20)

Note some aspects of the context, before we focus on the church's mission. Jesus commissions His disciples, first of all, because God has granted Him all authority in heaven and on earth. The disciples are worshiping Him, fulfilling the church's purpose. Jesus promises His presence, "always, to the very end of the age." He means to be present continually in His church. His authority and His presence together indicate that His power is active in this task. And, yes, Jesus has the church in mind, for He refers to the baptizing of disciples, one of the traditional biblical "marks" of the church. Any fulfillment of this Great Commission will involve the church.

He tells the church to do three things: make disciples, baptize them, and teach them to obey Christ's commands.

Let's talk about making disciples. We commonly equate "making disciples" with converting people to Christ. We also call it "discipling" when one believer helps another believer grow spiritually through individual teaching and modeling. But the Bible leads us to apply the term much more broadly. The church is to disciple everyone it meets. To disciple is to seek to influence someone else to accept Christian beliefs, namely the truth of the Word of God. Every time the Word influences the world, society, culture, families, or individuals, because a church or church member has communicated it, we should refer to it as discipling. This is what it means to be the salt of the earth (Matt. 5:13). The church salts the earth in both ways that ordinary table salt is typically used: it makes righteousness *tasty,* and it *preserves* righteousness. We are to live winsomely righteous lives, making righteousness tasty to the world around us. And we are to use our influence to preserve righteousness in our society. When discipling is conceived of in this way, it encompasses just about all our interactions with the watching world.

As with the church's purpose, so also with its mission: while every church embraces the same mission, each individual church will inevitably express that mission uniquely, due to the uniqueness of its community and its place in history and in culture. Keep this in mind as you ponder these examples, and as you think about your own church.

I recall a church whose aging members' pensions were funded by the local tobacco industry. They refused to concern themselves with social and moral conditions, wanting simply to maintain their own "spiritual ghetto." A church cannot do this and have an effect on the surrounding world.

As individuals and congregations disciple, they can be confident that God can and will use their influence to bring some of those people to know Him as Lord and Savior. Evangelism thus constitutes an integral and natural part of discipling.

Many wonderful things are happening now to involve all kinds of Christians in world missions. More and more suburban churches are offering opportunities for members to minister outside their own church. Short-term missions teams make this possible, whether to the inner city or to just about any country around the world. These ministries range from preaching to construction. Concrete ministries of mercy such as crisis pregnancy counseling or prison visitation also involve members beyond the bounds of the suburbs. As a result, individual believers experience and demonstrate much more vitality and power in their personal lives, at work, and at home.

This increasing global concern enhances the health of the churches that participate.

Discipling does not stop with conversion, but continues for the new believer. Other believers (the church) must help the newcomer learn and apply the same concepts from Scripture as God enables him or her to accept the Word of God as the final standard for faith and life.

As I said before, Jesus commands that new disciples be baptized, which means that He wants the church to be involved in discipling. The church baptizes new believers *into* God the Father, the Son, and the Holy Spirit. Baptism signifies union with God. The new believer belongs no longer to the World, but to Christ. He or she has been set apart to obey God's Word, to "purify ourselves from everything that contaminates body and spirit, perfecting holiness out of reverence for God" (2 Cor. 7:1).

The church must teach new believers to obey everything Christ has commanded. The church must have a multifaceted Christian education ministry. Its purpose is not merely to expand our knowledge of the Word of God. Christian education must continually reapply Scripture to our ever-changing cultural situation. And it must constantly call individual believers to decision after decision to obey Christ's commands, glorifying and enjoying God in more and more areas of life.

Every evangelical local church shares the same definition, the same purpose, and the same mission. But this does not mean that every church will look like every other church! In addition to divergent historical experiences and perspectives through which God has shaped an array of denominational points of view, one important characteristic distinguishes each local church. As we'll see in later chapters, each church has a vision that is all its own. Each congregation's vision is its particular concrete method of accomplishing the church's universal purpose and mission, utilizing its unique set of spiritual gifts and bringing the gospel to bear on the unique needs of its community at its particular time in history.

Every congregation, in order to carry out the church's universal purpose and mission, must specify its vision concretely. This is why I consider vision implementation one of the six healthy practices of a church. We'll discuss this concept more fully in part 3.

Essential Elements of the Church

Careful study of the book of Ephesians—something I recommend heartily to beginning churches—reveals certain essential elements of a church. To be missing any one of these is to fall short of being a church. I trust that most readers will find these to be obvious. Nevertheless, it is important that we affirm them.

Built of believers. First, the church consists of people whom God Himself has chosen and redeemed, in whom His Spirit is working. This is the message of Ephesians 1. To be part of a church, a person must have turned from rebellion against God, confessed this sin, and trusted Christ to save him from God's judgment. This person is now "in Christ," and has been made a "new creation" (2 Cor. 5:17). It is believers whom the Spirit is building into God's dwelling. "Once you were not a people, but now you are the people of God; once you had not received mercy, but now you have received mercy" (1 Peter 2:10). These are the "living stones" with which God is building a "spiritual house" (2:5).

We hope there will be people who join with us in worship

services and programs who have not yet become people of God. But we must never enlarge God's church by including un-believers as members. We must always take care to accept as members only those who have explicitly professed faith in Je-sus Christ and His good news. If a church fails to do this, its spiritual power will dissipate, along with its distinctive reason for existence.

I saw this happening in a large church that invited me to address them. In the past, this church had paid dearly to de-fend the gospel and the authority of Scripture, both in emo-tional stress and in actual dollars. When they separated from a mainline denomination because of these convictions, they were taken to court over property ownership, and in the end had to buy back their own property. As a result, the church had a good reputation as a stronghold of the faith.

But while I was there, I was invited to observe a meeting af-ter the worship service in which the elders interviewed prospective members. The prospective members were simply asked to state their name, address, and telephone number! Then an elder moved that they be accepted as members.

As you can guess, that made me question whether their ear-lier stand had been motivated by spiritual conviction or social comfort. I also predicted that what spiritual strength they had would eventually dissipate. Time has borne this out, as this church has not continued to evidence clear commitment on key issues.

Founded on Scripture. A second essential element is that God's church is built on one foundation alone. That founda-tion is "the apostles and prophets, with Christ Jesus himself as the chief cornerstone" (Eph. 2:20). This phrase refers not simply to the people who "started" the church, but also to their teaching. The church confesses that what they taught is true, that it is what we believe. The church confesses Scripture's authority as God's self-revelation, without error in the original manuscripts, and the only rule for faith and life. A church that no longer holds to the standard of the teaching of Christ, the prophets, and the apostles is, simply put, no longer a church.

Empowered by the Holy Spirit. Third, the church is enlivened by the work of the Holy Spirit. The Spirit brings spiritual life to believers, marking them for redemption (Eph. 1:14). The teaching of Christ, the prophets, and the apostles constitutes the very sword of the Spirit (Eph. 6:17). Thus, the Holy Spirit's work is evident in the first two essential elements of the church. But, thirdly, it is the Holy Spirit's power that brings any change, both in our individual lives and in the spiritual organism which is the church. Ephesians speaks of the "incomparably great power for us who believe" (1:19). This is the Spirit. The Holy Spirit, with resurrection power, brings dead people to life. The Holy Spirit also works to knit individual believers together into a church. He gives spiritual gifts to each member (4:7–13). He effects unity, building us into God's dwelling (2:11–22). He causes us to mature spiritually, until we attain to "the whole measure of the fullness of Christ" (4:13). Without the powerful working of the Holy Spirit, we are not a church.

The marks of the church. The Protestant Reformers of the church in the sixteenth century identified three marks of the church: the preaching of the Word, the administering of the sacraments, and the exercising of church discipline. In significant measure, these marks set off the church in much the same way as the elements we have just mentioned. A church that preaches the Scripture in its fullness, which administers the sacraments as a means for the Spirit to nurture His life in us, and which disciplines to the end of including believers and excluding unbelievers, is a true church as I have described it.

The Four Functions of a Church

Let us return briefly to our analogy of the church to a human body, both in the pursuit of health. Any human body can be expected to perform certain functions. It must keep getting itself fed. It must carry out desires. It must reflect rationally on its activity. Whatever its purpose or mission, the human body should be functioning in all these areas to remain living. Should one of these functions be absent, we would quite rightly infer that something has gone terribly awry.

Similarly, the church body can be expected to function in certain basic ways. The church's purpose and mission must be expressed in the four basic functions of *worship, nurture, mercy,* and *outreach*. If the church's purpose is to be the presence of Christ on earth, experiencing His perfecting work and leading the earth in His praise, and if its mission is the Great Commission, then the church should be carrying out these four functions as it pursues its purpose and mission.

Worship is that explicit praise of God for which the church exists. Nurture consists of the church's ministries, used by the Holy Spirit, to move individual believers and the body as a whole toward spiritual maturity. Mercy, the church's efforts to meet the physical needs of hurting people around the world, imitates Christ and carries out His command to give food and drink and clothing and medicine—for "whatever you did for one of the least of these brothers of mine, you did for me" (Matt. 25:40). In doing this, the church clearly images Christ before the watching world. Outreach is the mission of the church.

The Practices *of a* **Healthy** Church

A healthy church performs all four of these functions simultaneously. At any particular time, however, one function may be emphasized more than the others. For example, in a time of physical disaster, such as floods, earthquakes, tornadoes, and so on, a church quite rightly devotes itself extensively to ministries of mercy. In connection with a missions or evangelistic emphasis, a church should concentrate its energies on outreach. Planting a new church in a new neighborhood calls for plenty of outreach, while a church full of new Christians must emphasize nurture.

Worship. Worship, I believe, must in all circumstances be preserved and continually deepened. A church can easily feel pressured to put other priorities ahead of worship. We want to reach our community, so we replace the worship service with a "seeker" service. We have a building program underway, so we devote fifteen minutes to promoting the fund drive.

Corporate prayer should be included in worship. Along with worship, prayer taps us into divine resources without which a church might as well be the Junior League. We all know how easy it is to scrimp on prayer!

The fact that you have a worship service and a prayer meeting listed weekly on your church calendar does not necessarily guarantee that your church is performing these functions to a healthy degree. Stop and think: does your worship service truly involve believers actively in sacrificial praise to God? Is God Himself present and at work at these times, inhabiting the praise of His people, drawing near with comfort to those who confess their sins, and moving hearts through the preaching of the Word and the administering of the sacraments? Does the prayer meeting consist mostly of actual praying or mostly of Bible study or discussing requests? We'll see that elders are responsible to guard against well-meaning but dangerous pressure to weaken these functions.

Nurture. Nurture includes fellowship, instruction, the regular celebration of the sacraments, discipling, discipline, and shepherding. Elders see to it that the church continually challenges members to grow spiritually, to "put off your old self" and "be made new" (Eph. 4: 22–24). But the manner in which this is carried out signals a key difference between a healthy church and an unhealthy one. We'll see in later chapters that in a healthy church, members perceive that elders are shepherding them; in a less healthy church, members perceive that elders want them to change their ideas and practices to conform to Scripture, but they do not at the same time perceive that the elders are shepherding them. Where shepherding is absent, among other things, members do not profit from the natural motivation to change afforded by a mutually loving relationship.

Sadly, this is often the reality. Churches Vitalized surveyed eleven churches (1,200 respondents) and found that 69 percent stated that they expected their elders to urge them to change personal ideas and practices in order to conform to biblical standards, while 80 percent did not believe that their elders shepherded them. Now the elders in those churches were not heartless! I interviewed them, one by one. But either they struggled to meet urgent demands, which crowded out their prior responsibility to nurture the congregation, or they needed to learn how to serve as shepherds.

Some churches are unhealthy because the so-called spiritual leadership never challenges members to grow spiritually. In some of these churches, members begin to grow spiritually apart from the elders' leadership, often through their own personal study of the Word or through the influence of a parachurch ministry. But this creates a dynamic that can undermine the leadership. Although individual spiritual growth is a good thing, overall church health will suffer until elders assume the spiritual, shepherd leadership that God intends them to exercise.

We'll address these all too common problems extensively in part 2. For I believe the Bible shows how to make shepherding work—which is, of course, another way for your church to be healthy.

Mercy. Ministries of mercy should address the physical needs of the immediate church family, the community, and the world. It is important to include mercy as one of the essential functions of the church in order to prevent it from being overlooked. Evangelical churches often focus exclusively on evangelism and tend to forget ministries of mercy, no doubt because of the ultimate urgency of salvation as over against the temporality of physical needs. Some suggest that ministries of mercy should properly be regarded as the context for the church's entire ministry. Although this is true, if mercy is not singled out as a ministry in its own right, it too often becomes invisible. Still other people suggest that mercy be considered a part of outreach. For the same reason, I disagree: specifying mercy as an independent and essential function keeps us from overlooking it or giving it short shrift, something that we seem to be prone to do. A church with ministries of mercy, when suffering from a budget crunch, may ax this function first. But to do this is to forget the Lord Jesus' unmistakable message: "The King will say to those on his right, 'Come, you who are blessed by my Father; take your inheritance, the kingdom prepared for you since the creation of the world. For I was hungry and you gave me something to eat'" (Matt. 25:34–35).

Outreach. Outreach includes evangelism, missions, and what I call "being salty"—leading righteous lives that are tasty to the world around us, as well as attempting to preserve righteousness by taking a stand for biblical principles in an anti-Christian culture. With both functions, mercy and outreach, it is possible for a church to talk about doing these things and at the same time not be practicing them! Here is one place where the reality can be different from the perception, and where the reality matters and the perception doesn't!

When I was working with my denomination's church-planting agency, a group of young adults asked for help to establish a church. They had recently graduated from a large university, where they had been together in a campus ministry, and they eagerly set about to become a church body. But after nine months, they seemed to reach a plateau.

They asked for my counsel. It did not take long to recognize the problem. They had deep and impressive worship services. They took seriously their commitment to nurture families through Christian education. In adult Sunday school classes, more often than not the teacher referred to original Bible languages! They had a close network of mercy and support for each other and for the university community. They talked and prayed about evangelism. But, it became apparent, they did not practice evangelism. They were using three cylinders to run a four-cylinder ministry. As with this church, often the answer lies, not in reshaping intentions, but in accepting the challenge to reorganize programs to correspond to biblical priorities, and to exercise the faith it takes to be obedient.

Every church must engage in worship, nurture, mercy, and outreach at all times. But it's useful to realize that circumstances may from time to time shift the relative intensity with which we exercise these functions. For instance, when the St.

Louis area experienced catastrophic flooding in 1993, churches whose buildings and whose members' homes or businesses suffered damage, as well as churches that could offer resources to the community, responded mercifully with money, supplies, manpower, and shelter, matching special ministries to special crises. But they did not during that time forsake their other functions.

For a church to be healthy, it must strive to express the presence of Christ on earth. It must seek to disciple, baptize, and teach all nations. And it must be expressing its purpose and mission in its fourfold function: worship, nurture, mercy, and outreach.

Life, Ministry, and Structure: Facets of Church Life

To prepare to think about the practices of church health, we need to see the church in terms of one more set of categories. These bear directly on the rest of our discussion. For when I assess a church's health, I examine certain facets of church life. You'll be able to judge your church's health in terms of these facets, too. The six practices of church health relate specifically to these key facets. And when a church begins to spell out the implications of its unique vision, it must grasp how its vision ought to shape these facets.

To use our analogy of the human body, let's say that facets are like body parts. To be a body, we must have, for example, a heart, bones, and flesh. We can match critical facets of the church to these anatomical requirements.

When you think about what makes up a church, a couple of obvious things come to mind. First, there is a *building*. As in the rhyme, "Here is the church; here is the steeple; open the doors and see all the people," the "church" is often identified with tangible facilities. Our facilities do represent a tangible facet of our church, but not a primary one.

Another tangible facet that comes to mind is *staff*—people on our church's payroll, or official volunteers. The person or persons we might identify with our church are the people employed by it, paid or unpaid.

Of course, we've learned our Bible lessons well enough to know that we should rather identify the church with the rhyme's fingers wagging inside—the people! There are three less tangible and more critical facets of any church, and they all have to do with the people, the church body as a whole: they are *life, ministry,* and *structure.* If you really want to capture the essence of a church, you must describe these three facets. Suppose you and your family have just moved to a new town and are looking for a new church. What would you most like to know about a church in order to assess it? And once you've become a part of it, what "inside information" will make you feel as if you really know your church?

The central question you'll want to answer is this: is this church *spiritually alive?* Is God vibrantly at work among these people? Are lives being changed, unbelievers coming to Christ, believers growing in their faith, and brokenness being healed in the name of Jesus? Or is it a lifeless church? Life is perhaps the most critical facet of a church, the one that indicates most directly the health of a body. It indicates the presence of the essential ingredient: God!

Another important question is this: what *ministries* is this church involved in? This includes the activities you might see listed in a bulletin or brochure about the church. What does the church do when it meets together? How does it carry out worship, nurture, mercy, and outreach?

The third facet is one you may not immediately think of,

but which has a lot to do with the character of a church. This facet is *structure*—the authority structure, to be more precise. Each denomination specifies a certain formal structure. But what I have in mind as most critical is the unspecified structure, the infrastructure.

Who's "king of the mountain"? Is there an unofficial pecking order, a chain of command and communication? If people in the ministries of the church would do something "because so-and-so says so," who would that so-and-so be? Is it the pastor? The treasurer? A voting congregation? A certain family or clan? Are there competing factions? The evangelism task force? The counseling center? The elders? The Lord?

Once you've identified the informal chain of command, you can ask a further question: what styles of leadership and influence are being employed by the people in these key connections? Suppose there really is a match between the officially designated leaders and the unofficially followed leaders. How is that leadership being carried out? Are leaders "telling everybody what to do"? Or are the leaders doing everything themselves? Or are they helping the people to be involved in a significant way? It's easy to see that styles of leadership significantly shape a church. Granted, spiritual life may be the most important of the three critical facets of a church. But if something is awry with its infrastructure—if it fails to conform to Scripture's directives—then no vibrant life, despite its origin in the work of the Holy Spirit, can be sustained for any length of time.

Life, ministry, and structure. If you picture the church as a human body, you might think of life as the body's heart, ministry as its flesh, and structure as its skeleton. Facilities and staff, perhaps, could be likened to clothing—something secondary. For as we address the health of life, ministries, and structure, issues concerning facilities and staff will be solved as well.

Health must characterize each of these facets. The six practices of health described in this book will enable your church to assess and enhance health on all three fronts.

Healthy *life* includes demonstrating the presence of Christ before the watching world (this chapter). It includes living communication from God as His Word is preached and maintained in purity as the defining characteristic of every ministry in the church (chapter 3). It includes dynamic worship and prayer, enabling the ongoing vibrant relationship of individuals and the group to their living Lord, whose sovereign love motivates all our response (chapter 4). It includes a spiritual, shepherding relationship between elders and members.

Healthy *ministry* involves accomplishing the church's functions (worship, nurture, mercy, and outreach), its purpose and mission as expressed in its unique vision, in such a way that internal resources and dynamics, as well as community needs and opportunities, are strategically utilized or addressed (see especially chapters 5, 8, 9, and 10).

Healthy *structure* accommodates both of the Bible's injunctions: a church's elders are accountable to God for its people, even as its members' Spirit-bestowed gifts are strategically utilized. The people must share significantly in decision making. Elders must think of themselves, not as members of a board of directors, but as shepherds (chapters 5, 6, 8, 9, and 10).

We'll see that as a church family formulates and adopts a specific vision that addresses both the health of these facets and the concrete manner in which it will carry out the church's universal purpose and mission, the proper nature and role of the church's staff and facilities will fall into place. Both staff and facilities should be thought of as resources rather than results, as means rather than ends. How do we utilize them optimally? How do we reshape them to serve new needs and opportunities in our congregation and in our community? We should avail ourselves of what they offer, without allowing them to hinder us from taking further steps that God may be calling us to take (chapter 10).

God's church is the very presence of Christ on earth between His advents, the voice of creation offering praise to Him, His designated agent for discipling the nations, the bride He sovereignly selected, redeemed at ultimate cost to Himself, and is now sparing no expense to perfect. This marvelous institution compels our wonder and calls for our allegiance. To pursue its health is to share in the Lord's gracious, redemptive agenda. We are His grateful beneficiaries; we are also His chosen instruments.

Healthy Body Life Begins with Prayer

Whenever a church asks me to help them assess and reshape their life, ministry, and structure, I make them sign a covenant before I ever agree to help. I ask them to sign a covenant *to pray.* This praying must be ongoing for as long as I partner with them, but hopefully for the rest of that church's life on earth. I specify that this prayer be filled with content. I suggest that they list on paper each of the church's four functions, each of the church's programs as they relate to these functions, and each program's key coordinator. Then they must regularly pray for each program and its coordinator by name. They must also pray for all paid members of staff and their families, for the church's financial affairs, for the physical plant, and for any unusual circumstances or challenges (including my ministry and their implementation of my recommendations!).

This prayer ministry requires a prayer coordinator, a mechanism whereby this praying will take place regularly, volunteers who will pray, and a computer to generate a continually updated chart that displays the church's programs under the headings of worship, nurture, mercy, and outreach.

If your church is like many others, organized prayer times generally focus on individuals' spiritual and physical needs, with relatively little attention being given to the life and ministry of the church. But if we want God to work spiritual wellness in our church body, we can only expect that to occur as we embrace the endeavor and bathe it in prayer. Concrete prayer expresses our belief that God and God alone will effect corporate spiritual growth and maturity. Concrete prayer invokes His divine power to this end, and it shapes and sharpens our focus on the task at hand.

When your church is praying in this focused manner, it is fulfilling its function of worship. On your chart of functions and their programs, you can list the prayer program—and pray for it, too! Focused prayer also counts as part of the church's ministry, and it should deepen the church's life.

Generating a chart of the church's functions and programs and praying over it bring to our attention any superfluous overlapping of ministry, as well as any gaps. We will attend to these as we reshape our vision.

Find a concrete way to pray for your church. See to it that you all, between you, uphold every program in prayer, continually beseeching God for His divine power, which alone will shape your church into a blemish-free, wrinkle-free, healthy, adoring body that evidences Christ on earth. It's the step you need to take now, even before you read the rest of this book, for it is the crucial first step that begins the journey of a church's lifetime.

Questions for Discussion

1. Study the Bible passages about the church quoted in this chapter. In what ways does your church reflect the biblical picture of temple, body, and bride?

2. How does your community perceive your church? In what ways could you improve their perception of you as the presence of Christ on earth? How can we avoid a fortress mentality or a maintenance mentality?

3. In what ways do your church's members disciple others by being salty in your community—preserving righteousness and making it tasty?

4. How does your church fulfill the four functions of worship, nurture, outreach, and mercy? Do these receive even treatment?

5. Is your church regularly praying for its ministries, seeking God for His blessing? If not, what sorts of things are you praying for, and how regularly?

Chapter 3 The Bible: The Hallmark of a Healthy Church

Healthy Practice #1: The church must retain its commitment to the Holy Scriptures without compromise.

When I speak of the Bible as the hallmark of the church, I mean that a church's defining characteristic should always be the faithful use of the Bible, God's holy and inerrant Word.

In one key way, this healthy practice is the most difficult one to write about. The problem is that just about every evangelical church likes to think that in this respect at least it is a healthy church, with no need for adjustment. My first task is to keep you from skipping this chapter!

However, a church's commitment to the Word of God *in principle* may not be matched by its commitment *in practice*. This mismatch may characterize all or part of a church's life and ministry. It's easy to admit the abstract possibility; it takes an objectivity granted by the grace of God to see one's own defect in this area. Are we Bible-oriented? Of course we're Bible-oriented! The sermon is forty-five minutes long; Sunday school for all ages lasts an hour; we have small-group studies and a Christian grade school! You are right to point to these critical ministries, but the Bible is not thereby shown to be the hallmark of your church.

Various things may usurp the Bible's place of supremacy: a particular system of theology, a particular doctrine, a particular code of behavior, a particular person's teaching ministry, a particular style of worship, a particular style of Christian living, a particular church ministry (such as counseling or a Christian school), the preserving of a particular social or ethnic homogeneity, a commitment to political power or influence, a commitment to a particular political agenda, or a commitment to extrabiblical self-evaluative criteria (such as the advice of financial experts or sociological analysts). It is quite possible to offer Bible programs and at the same time harbor one of these usurpers.

You can imagine a church in which a particular doctrine or doctrinal system reigns supreme. That doctrine would really be more important than the Bible, or at least more important than the rest of the Bible. It might become the standard of orthodoxy, a test informally administered to leaders and congregants alike. It might shape all of the Bible programs in the church.

You can imagine what happens when a particular person's teaching is elevated above the Bible. What is it about your church that you all want to promote? What is it about the kingdom of God that you want to promote? A particular person's teaching? This scenario has its own biblical precedent: the Corinthian church was bickering over which leader to follow (1 Cor. 3). What ministry of your church ranks foremost? Does it eclipse in some measure the preaching of the whole Bible? Are most, if not all forays into the Bible shaped by that ministry, with passages chosen and interpreted to support a single cause?

The question really has to do with the first of the Ten Commandments: "You shall have no other gods before me." The alternative is called idolatry. As individuals, we are always fighting the battle against usurpers, other candidates for worship in our lives: our social status, our possessions, our children, our job. We may have slid into idolatry without noticing it. We must continually scrutinize our outlook, our motivation, and our commitments, to see whether they evidence a supreme commitment to God alone, outclassed by no other "god."

It's the same dynamic, but on the corporate church level, which now concerns us. Just as we scrutinize ourselves as individuals, so we should scrutinize ourselves as a church body. To countenance one or more usurpers is to practice a form of idolatry. Correcting such a problem can only enhance a church's spiritual health.

Even the most healthy churches must continually scrutinize themselves on this matter. You should not take the act of self-scrutiny as an admission of guilt, or even as one that sets you apart from other churches! As the doctor replied to the patient who was shocked by a positive result on the pregnancy test, "My dear, all of us are 'that kind of girl'!" Our sinful propensities drag us, individually and corporately, into idolatry, just as our physical bodies continually deteriorate. Health requires ongoing self-scrutiny. "Therefore, dear friends, since you already know this, be on your guard so that you may not be carried away by the error of lawless men and fall from your secure position. But grow in the grace and knowledge of our Lord and Savior Jesus Christ. To him [alone!] be glory both now and forever!" (2 Peter 3:17–18).

In this chapter, I hope to help you in this process by doing three things. First, I want to look more closely at one particular usurper, to aid you in making the distinction I have in mind and in accurately assessing your own church. I choose to address the ascendancy of a theological position or doctrine over the Bible, because this particular candidate has in my own circles been both the most popular and the least easy to detect. Churches need to make sure that the Bible, as opposed to a particular theological stance or systematization of doctrine, serves as their hallmark. Ultimately, Scripture and doctrine should not be in opposition to one another. I speak rather of focus. But we must be wise enough to make this distinction, for giving priority to a doctrine or doctrinal system over God's Word is wrong, and it is unhealthy. Whether our church does this intentionally or unintentionally, the effect is the same.

Second, I want to remind you of what is at stake in keeping the Bible as the hallmark of your church. The key member of our church leadership, to speak somewhat facetiously, is God! He communicates exclusively through the pages of His Word, as God the Holy Spirit works in our hearts. This avenue of communication must be guarded at all costs, for without it, we are simply not Christ's church. Maintaining the authority of the Bible involves us necessarily in active reliance on the Holy Spirit, who is both its author and its communicator. We must utilize Scripture in such a way that it expresses our continual and vital (in both senses!) dependence on Him.

Third, I wish to spell out three concrete ways to implement faithful use the Bible. First, Scripture must be seen to be both necessary and sufficient to effect personal and corporate spiritual growth. Second, we must ensure that Scripture shapes and imbues every ministry of our church. I will suggest some concrete ways to do this. Third, we must bring this sword of the Spirit (Eph. 6:17) to bear on the continually changing cultural situations in which God places the church. We must not hesitate to speak to people using the words of Scripture, even when we feel that we share little or no common ground. Scripture constitutes God's catalyst for change.

A church that wants to glorify God by pursuing health must understand and apply these things, exhibiting commitment to Scripture as its hallmark, not only on paper, but also in practice. In the previous chapter, we saw that Scripture constitutes the "foundation of the apostles and prophets," along with the teaching of Christ (the cornerstone), without which a church really could not be considered a church. In this chapter we see the matter stated positively: allegiance to the Bible produces good health. It makes you what you are as a church, and it also makes you better at what you're meant to be.

I hope that, whatever else you conclude after reading this book, you will be able to say without qualification: "The Bible has shaped MacNair's ideas." My primary intention is to take seriously and develop concretely what Scripture says about the church. Wherever you prick me, I might say, I am going to bleed the Bible! Yes, I bring a lot of experience to this discussion. But any amount of experience is significant only as it helps to understand and apply God's Word in greater depth. In the end, it is the God of the Bible who speaks and who alone has the words of life.

Just as my particular ministry to the church grows out of the teaching of Scripture, so should every ministry of every local church. What I have attempted to do in this book is what I call upon you to do in every facet of your church's ministry.

Psalm 23 Versus the Reformed Faith

Some years ago, after conducting a workshop on church health, I spoke with a minister who came forward. He was weeping quietly.

He told me that during his time in seminary, he had grasped the vital significance of the Reformed faith. In a homiletics class, he had raised the question of its role in his prospective ministry, especially in his preaching and teaching. He told the professor about the old and rather lifeless church that had recently called him as pastor. "What should characterize my preaching in order to lead the church into vitality?" he asked the professor.

"Preach the Reformed faith," the professor told him. "When people hear it, it will revolutionize them."

This pastor did just that. For the next ten years he made the Reformed faith the hallmark of his preaching and teaching. He taught and preached it as the revolutionary power that his church needed.

However, no move toward spiritual vitality ever occurred. Now he bitterly expressed his sad realization to me: "I wish someone had told me ten years ago to make the *Bible* the hallmark of my ministry!"

His woeful comment has haunted my thoughts and crystallized the subtle but critical distinction that we must make if we are to obey God and grow healthy as churches. We are to preach the Bible, not a system of doctrine.

Systematization is unavoidable. As soon as we have read enough in the Bible to compare or contrast different verses, grouping the ones that say similar things and using one to elucidate another, we are systematizing. Theological systems consist of the categories under which Scripture truths can be collected for further study, teaching, and discussion. Systems unavoidably suggest which passages and interpretations should be regarded as primary for any given doctrine, and which doctrines are more or less important.

Many believers naively think that it is possible to believe and teach the Bible while avoiding any particular doctrinal system. Such people can never be successful in the attempt. However sincere, this amounts to self-deception; for us to communicate at all, we must systematize.

Nor should we regard this systematization as inherently evil. We are not condemned to avoid the unavoidable. All knowledge advances by grouping and assessing; theology is no different. What is more, it is reasonable to believe that the Spirit expects and even guides this enterprise. Consider, for example, the apostle Paul's overpowering argument in Romans 3:9–18 to prove that no one is righteous: he cites one Old Testament passage after another, grouping them together in support of a key element in the gospel of Jesus Christ.

A theological system is useful, also. It gives us a way to relate one Scripture to another, and it enables us to relate the truth of Scripture to the issues of life. These are the proper uses of a system of beliefs.

For these reasons, my own denomination calls itself a "confessional church." This means that we acknowledge that some sort of system is both unavoidable and useful, and that in order to define what kind of church we are and believe God wants us to be, we subscribe to a particular confession, or system, of theology.

What we must avoid is an improper use of our system of beliefs. We use a theological system improperly if we consciously or unconsciously expect it to bring spiritual life. Scripture, and only Scripture, brings spiritual life.

For instance, when a loved one dies, the doctrinal system will help the bereaved one understand the trauma in the light of God's sovereign hand, but it is Psalm 23 which brings healing. If we are to minister healing, comforting words in that situation, we must speak God's words of Scripture rather than cite theological conclusions.

We easily fall prey to the temptation to idolize a doctrine or a system. That temptation is greatest directly after a Christian grasps that doctrine and begins to appreciate its implications for his or her life. Greater understanding is always exciting. As the believer masters its nuances, he or she may reason that even further application will allow us to make sense of everything.

A doctrinal system is like a tool. Having the right tool for a job brings sheer delight. But it would be a mistake to expect that tool to work for every other kind of job. To make the analogy more direct, it would be a mistake to spend our lives thinking about the usefulness of that tool, trying to use it in every circumstance.

There can be bad consequences. Inappropriate commitment to a particular doctrinal system or a particular doctrine fosters an attitude of superiority on the part of those who hold to it. They tend to believe and to intimate that they have "arrived" spiritually, that those who understand this doctrine belong to an elite class of Christians, and that those who don't are second-class. A person's having arrived is usually assessed in terms of his or her use of the proper buzzwords. Those of us who have encountered this mentality within a congregation know how divisive it can be.

There is a more serious and disastrous consequence: when this scenario unfolds, it reduces the Bible to a mere resource for proof texts to justify the doctrine. The tail thus wags the dog. And, in this case, the inevitable result is motion sickness. To elevate our doctrinal system to the authoritative role of Scripture is to forget that "the fear of the LORD is the beginning of wisdom, and knowledge of the Holy One is understanding" (Prov. 9:10). It cuts off the sole source of spiritual life.

Granted, unwavering emphasis on a key doctrine may at

first produce signs of a healthy church, including fast growth. But over the long haul, that growth will be stunted, for it undermines the ongoing work of the Spirit. He uses all of the Bible, over time, to increase our knowledge of God.

Granted, the more explicit and rigid a church's doctrinal commitment is, the easier it is for people to be like-minded. Anyone who seeks to join in will have to state explicitly the critical doctrines. But where an explicitly specified doctrinal stance prevails, the result is often a stern, hard-line church that is unattractive to, and without influence on, people outside the chosen group.

The problem here lies not with like-mindedness or with accountability to a confessional standard *per se*. Obviously, church leadership rightfully espouses both. The problem is with excessive rigidity. The specificity of a confessional agreement should not exceed the specificity of Scripture itself. It is appropriate, it is healthy, to allow for differing beliefs and applications where Scripture offers no contradiction.

Yes, it may be easier to relate to those who think exactly the way we do. But, in addition to drastically curtailing the number of people to whom we relate and thereby stunting the body's growth, this approach erodes the necessity to depend on the Spirit as we trust Him to use others beside those of our exact persuasion. I say this more thoroughly elsewhere, but it must be mentioned here: mutual trust—trust that God is using the gifts He has given to every member of our church for the common good—lubricates a church's working together.

Let me give you an example. Several years ago, I was part of a denomination that came into existence through passionately contesting false doctrine in its parent denomination. If any denomination had the Bible as its hallmark, surely our new denomination did! However, the passage of time revealed a more urgent commitment: what characterized us was the desire, above all else, to be separated from heretical denominational ties. Separation, rather than the whole counsel of God, became our hallmark. The problem was not with separation, but with its ascendancy over commitment to Scripture. The denomination was projecting a judgmental attitude to the watching world. Some churches felt uncomfortable with this ungracious demeanor, sensing that its offense to unbelievers was not exactly "the offense of the cross" (Gal. 5:11). Sadly, their only recourse was to leave the denomination, for it did not recognize any need to revise its outlook. One group after another split away, leaving the original group smaller and smaller. Other churches considered joining the denomination because of a common commitment to Scripture, but they were rejected as not sufficiently separate from perceived compromise.

Here is another example. I recall a church whose pastor began a series of sermons on the biblical doctrine of predestination. He had good reason to do so, since the doctrine was openly maligned in the area. The problem was that he kept on preaching on the subject for months, regardless of the biblical text or the theme of his message. A church split resulted. After years of struggle, neither of the fragmented bodies ever recovered and became a healthy church. I met with one of those churches. I found a small band of people who were apparently committed only to taking care of themselves. I asked them to consider reconciling. I asked them to try to understand their community and to reach out to it in light of a concrete vision, rather than continuing as a detraction. Both propositions were rejected.

Remember, I am not advocating an absence of doctrinal conviction! That would go against everything I stand for in my commitment to the authority of Scripture. Plus, as I have said, a systematized approach is not only unavoidable, but also good and useful. How is it possible to hit the happy medium? How does a church specify a doctrinal stance while avoiding the undesirable excesses?

We must remember at all times that our commitment is first and foremost to the Word and to the Spirit. No doctrinal tool should be allowed to usurp first place. We must remember to depend continually on the Holy Spirit to teach us how to understand His Word properly and how to apply it in new situations. We must determine what sorts of differences are minor and workable and what sorts of differences pose a threat to the central core of biblical doctrine. Scripture itself gives us no explicit criterion for deciding each and every such case. Such a guiding maxim can only be regarded as fallible and be held with humility, to be used only in conjunction with prayerful dependence on the Holy Spirit.

Obviously, this approach is not clear-cut or easy to regulate. But success using it reflects the graciousness of Christ and the freedom of life in Him. As it maintains dependence on the Spirit and mutual trust, it produces longer lasting church health.

Other Idols

Other facets of church life, many legitimate in themselves, can subtly or blatantly usurp the definitive role meant only for the Bible. Let me simply share a few experiences to document this.

I was engaged as consultant for a church of 2,500 people. One older woman told me that her father and grandfather had been elders in that church, that her husband was currently an elder, and that her son would someday be an elder, too. Would you agree with me that a dynamic other than commitment to Scripture defined that church?

I remember a church that devoted hours of session and committee time to debating a then-current political issue: whether or not the President of the United States should have a seat at the United Nations. I can think of a formal association of churches that expended a good deal of energy attempting to convince the country of its size and thus its qualification to represent people formally in Washington, D.C. Both of these exemplify a heavier commitment to political concerns than to the ministry of the Word of God.

I worked with one conservative, Bible-believing church that had a massive commitment to a counseling ministry. The church was concerned that, while many people from the community would come and visit the church, few would stay and join. Several factors were involved. But it became apparent to me that newcomers never really got the impression that the church was concerned with anything other than counseling. Had the Bible and its ministry been truly the church's hallmark, newcomers would have sensed that the church put them in touch, not so much with their problems, but with the living God. The church had never intended this, nor was it aware of the subtle shift of emphasis. What they were doing was worthwhile, but their church failed to evidence the dynamic vitality of spiritual health.

In response to this assessment, the church wrote a vision statement in which counseling remained a cornerstone, but was reconstrued as a service ministry supporting the church and its central commitment to Scripture. I also proposed that the church grant the pastor a leave of absence to develop a professional counseling center. Once established, this would free his ministry to include more than the pulpit counseling he had continually felt obligated to do. The church took these steps of faith, and the recovered balance has issued in robust health.

Some aspects of the church-growth movement have substituted another hallmark for the Bible. What I have in mind is a bottom-line commitment to principles drawn from anthropology or sociology, rather than from Scripture. Here again, we recognize a factor in church ministry that, while legitimate in itself, becomes illegitimate if weighted more heavily than the Bible. A study that examines the ten most successful Sunday schools, looking for common denominators so that you can make yours work, has not put the Bible first. This leads to the practice of evaluating your church according to nonbiblical standards.

This approach should be replaced with a totally new premise: the biblical concept that the church is not product-driven, but process-driven. The product lies in God's hands alone. We should commit ourselves to maintaining the process, starting with keeping His living message, the Word, supreme as our source of spiritual health and life, our criterion for self-evaluation, and our guide for healthy practice.

One last illustration: worship style. Scripture dictates the elements that any worship of God must include: praise, prayer, confession of sin, music, preaching of the Word, the sacraments. However, Scripture does not dictate the style of worship, and here I have in mind the spectrum of possibilities from traditional to contemporary worship, liturgical to informal. A church that insists on a certain style thus adopts a degree of commitment more rigid and restrictive than Scripture itself. It is certainly fine—in fact, unavoidable—that a particular church has a certain style. Factors that influence a choice of style include that church's own resources, its vision, and the surrounding community. But when the style outweighs Scripture in importance—when the primary justification is, "We've always done it that way" or "We can't use a drum or a guitar on Sunday morning" (or perhaps an organ!) or "We have to wear dress clothes" (or jeans!)—we should sense a rival to the Bible as our hallmark and strive to reassert its purity and centrality.

The Spirit of the Word

Our goal must be to use the Bible faithfully in our lives and in every ministry of the church. In the next section, we'll look at positive ways to use the Bible faithfully. But before that, let's take a moment to reflect further on the role of the Holy Spirit in connection with the Bible.

So often we overlook His role. We need to be reminded regularly. And we can expect that people in the pews will need to be taught how to depend on the Spirit in the faithful use of Scripture.

To use the Bible faithfully in ministry, we must enunciate its truths. We must be convinced of its authoritative relevance to any situation. And we must spell out its implications for daily living and for the new problems that we constantly face.

The Holy Spirit's twofold role in regard to Scripture makes both of these possible. He authored the Word; He also guides our application of it.

The Bible is God's revelation by Himself of Himself. The apostle Peter explains the process: "No prophecy of Scripture came about by the prophet's own interpretation. For prophecy never had its origin in the will of man, but men spoke from God as they were carried along by the Holy Spirit" (2 Peter 1:19–21). Peter makes it clear that the Bible is the written

Word of God (even as Jesus is the living Word of God). God the Holy Spirit must be counted as the author of record, for He "carried along" human writers in such a way that they spoke God's very words.

With the very words of God available to us, they obviously must carry supreme authority. These words constitute the very foundation of the church. Without these words, there would be no religious authority—no church. Period. The church submits to the Word of God in all things.

But the Holy Spirit was not finished when the Bible was completed. His ongoing role of illumination is one that we often overlook, perhaps because we fail to understand its necessity. But it is His illuminating work that our faithful use of Scripture requires.

Any teacher who has thought about teaching and learning realizes that simply to have uttered a true statement in no way guarantees that a hearer will learn it. The job of communicating is only partly underway with the utterance. An utterance without the hearer's appropriation of it is like an electric lamp without a cord—useless!

The Holy Spirit created the electric lamp, so to speak; He also plugs it in. The word *illumination* suggests this metaphor. Without His illuminating ministry, the circuit cannot be completed. With it, we understand Scripture and can apply it to our experience.

Paul makes it clear that, although people have the revelation of God as the foundation to start with, they cannot then go off into their own subjective notions of what it says and how it applies to faith and practice. Rather, they must follow the Spirit's guidance for the necessary help to understand it. Paul says, "We speak of God's secret wisdom. . . . None of the rulers of this age understood it . . . but God has revealed it to us by his Spirit" (1 Cor. 2:7–10a). He says that "the Spirit searches all things, even the deep things of God" (v. 10b); that we have "received . . . the Spirit who is from God, that we may understand what God has freely given us" (v. 12), and that "this is what we speak . . . in words taught by the Spirit, expressing spiritual truths in spiritual words" (v. 13).

The inevitable systematization that we spoke of earlier must, therefore, also be pursued under the guidance of the Holy Spirit. We must look to the Spirit to teach us, to implant the truth in our lives, so that we express it by the way we live. We must depend on the Holy Spirit to shape our sermons, and to graft the message onto the hearts of hearers. That is why we pray as we prepare and as we begin to preach. Not only pastors and teachers must pray; hearers must pray, too. And both speaker and hearer must pray for both speaker and hearer. Perhaps we think of the Spirit's role more readily in the context of conversion; but a little reflection helps us recognize our dependence on Him for any successful communication of God's truth.

Of course, Scripture does not teach that our sermons and our systems are infallible. Perhaps it is thinking this way that can lead us to venerate a system over Scripture. This is the opposite of depending on the Spirit and His inscripturated Word. At no point are we ever able to stop learning, stop depending on the Spirit, and begin thinking we've arrived in our understanding. This ongoing dependence must be borne out in the manner in which we treat the Word: we seek the Lord's help to teach us and others, we seek it in every circumstance in which we apply the Word, and we seek to apply the Word in every circumstance.

He never cuts the umbilical cord. He did not intend to. Nor should we.

Faithfully Using Scripture in All Things

God's Word has supreme authority. The Holy Spirit enables us to understand and apply it. Next, He expects us to use His Word.

Scripture tells us of its own power. God Himself has promised: "So is my word that goes out from my mouth: It will not return to me empty, but will accomplish what I desire and achieve the purpose for which I sent it" (Isa. 55:11). No other book carries such an awesome guarantee!

Such a powerful tool is meant to be put to use. "All Scripture is God-breathed," Paul writes, "and is useful for teaching, rebuking, correcting and training in righteousness, so that the man of God may be thoroughly equipped for every good work" (2 Tim. 3:16–17). He calls the Word of God "the sword of the Spirit" (Eph. 6:17). A powerful person with a powerful sword is a force not to be underestimated!

This power is concentrated on the human heart—that seat of our being that shapes who we are and that determines our relationship to God—the heart which is "the wellspring of life" (Prov. 4:23). The writer of the book of Hebrews declares:

> For the word of God is living and active. Sharper than any double-edged sword, it penetrates even to dividing soul and spirit, joints and marrow [items that are so closely connected that it is humanly impossible to divide them]; it judges the thoughts and attitudes of the heart. Nothing in all creation is hidden from God's sight. Everything is uncovered and laid bare before the eyes of him to whom we must give account. (Heb. 4:12–13)

Human hearts before God can never maintain the status quo. Sinful, "deceitful above all things, and desperately wicked"

(Jer. 17:9 KJV), they cannot remain as they are and please God. Conversion represents one key step in a larger process. Remember that God means to cause us to mature spiritually, both as individuals and as a church body. He is continually beautifying His bride. This process is what growth and health are all about.

But for growth to occur, there must be change. It is the Word of God, the sword of the Spirit of God, which effects the change. It alone is necessary; by itself it is sufficient.

With so effective a tool at our disposal, why would we ever sheathe it? The obvious answer is that our sin makes us run from God's work. Plus, His healing does not always feel pleasurable. Like a doctor, He has limbs to amputate, cavities to fill, and wounds to cauterize, not to mention assigning an eating regimen that we might find unappetizing at first. This means that it will always take an effort to keep using the Word, the sword of the Spirit. And it will take continual persistence and creativity to apply it in more and more areas of life and ministry. This is what I have in mind when I speak of the *faithful* use of Scripture.

One qualification needs to be stated. To have the Bible as the hallmark of our church does not mean simply that we talk a lot about the Bible, or even that we talk all the time about the Bible. It is possible to talk a lot about the Bible and not really *use* it, let alone use it faithfully! We must be sure in our talking about the Bible that we are in fact applying it to the ever-fresh situations in which we find ourselves. These situations include personal experiences, life in the family and in the community, church affairs, and encounters with prevailing cultural ideas. One might think that a list of Sunday school classes that all deal with books of the Bible would evidence that we are people of the Word. In fact, however, we may not be using the Word faithfully, for we may be failing to apply it to every area of life. On the other hand, a class list including classes on parenting, work, philosophy, and counseling might demonstrate a desire to apply Scripture faithfully to all areas of life.

Personal Spiritual Food

In particular, we must expect to use Scripture faithfully on three levels—the personal, the corporate, and the cultural. Let me show you what it takes for the Bible to be the defining hallmark of a church.

A healthy church encourages members to use Scripture in personal and family devotions. The Bible's longest chapter (176 verses) is Psalm 119, a poem written exclusively to show that the Word of God is life itself, central to all that is good, the answer to all human problems. Its author, apparently a young man surrounded by unbelievers, trouble, and pain, expresses repeatedly his devotion to God's Word and his dependence on it. If our hearts are our most basic "mouth," craving to be fed, the Word is our most basic, most satisfying food. A few verses of the psalm suffice to show that the Lord blesses us when we learn, honor, and obey His revelation:

> How can a young man keep his way pure?
> By living according to your word.
> I seek you with all my heart;
> do not let me stray from your commands.
> I have hidden your word in my heart
> that I might not sin against you.
> Praise be to you, O LORD;
> teach me your decrees.
> With my lips I recount
> all the laws that come from your mouth.

I rejoice in following your statutes
    as one rejoices in great riches.
I meditate on your precepts
    and consider your ways.
I delight in your decrees;
    I will not neglect your word. (vv. 9–16)

No doubt remains in the reader's mind that God means His Word to be our heart's desire, our spiritual food. We know God through His Word and through His Word alone. For God to have first place in our lives, His Word must occupy first place as spiritual food. Because He spoke this self-revelation, we can always communicate with Him. Through it, the Spirit brings change, as He pierces to the dividing of soul and spirit.

Personal spiritual growth undergirds the overall growth of a church body toward spiritual maturity. If individual members are not growing spiritually, it is impossible for a church to mature. Therefore, the church must see to it that the Word is taught and preached in such a way that the Holy Spirit can use it, His one and only tool, to effect spiritual change in hearers' hearts. The sermon or lesson must presume the need for the Spirit's work; it must presume that the Word is the agent of that work; it must presume that such change is occurring and will continue to occur. And this presumption must be evident in every ministry of the church.

People of the Word

What makes a particular church ministry outstanding? Whether it is evangelism, missions, mercy, or youth, we often assess it merely in terms of its size or budget. We may also judge it in terms of its efficiency and effectiveness. With this last consideration, we move closer to a proper criterion for a ministry. In the context of a church, with God's goals in mind, what else could "effective" mean than producing spiritual growth? For spiritual growth to be occurring, both the content and the overall goals of a ministry must reflect the influence of Scripture. Scripture should be seen to have shaped everything we plan and implement, as well as everything we teach and preach. And, in every respect, our dependence on the Holy Spirit must be deepening continually. Only by drawing on this resource will a ministry properly be called outstanding, and only thus will it grow in health.

The highest compliment a church could receive would be to be called "people of the Word." This should mean not only that we study Scripture, but also that we seek to apply it to our lives, our ministries, and our culture, and that we do so in dependence on the Holy Spirit.

How can we faithfully use the Bible in our church's ministries? Here are some concrete goals that church leaders can implement.

Every new program of the church must start with a specific goal or purpose that is derived from the Bible. References to Scripture that justify this new program can be used in the defining documents of the program. The program must be reviewed annually. This annual evaluation keeps the program on track, spiritually speaking. At times of review, we must ask whether the program is achieving its goals and conforms to Scripture. This keeps the program dependent on the Holy Spirit. Without the review, a ministry may become people-driven rather than Spirit-driven. It may exist only to feed itself, taking little notice of a growing discrepancy between itself and people's needs and spiritual gifts.

Existing programs, which began before people were aware

of the need to tie ministry to Scripture, must also have their scriptural orientation specified. Defining documents must also be written for these obvious, long-standing programs, because from this point on we must continually evaluate them to keep them on track.

We must also let biblical truths determine the shape that every program takes. The Bible also shapes our procedures for evaluation.

We should commit ourselves to using the Bible in all parts of every program, whenever it is feasible.

We should strive in our worship services, and especially in the preaching of the Word, to make the Bible a living expression of Jesus Christ. Our teaching must enable members to know their way around the Bible. It must challenge them to obey what the Bible says. It must equip them to ferret out and apply objective implications, and discourage them from making selective, subjective applications. But above all, hearers should walk away not simply having been chastised or commanded, not merely with more Bible content, but having met Christ afresh, having appropriated His forgiveness, provision, and power.

Elders must use the Bible as the basis for all aspects of their shepherding ministry, from decision making to addressing people's spiritual needs.

Whatever you attempt, always evaluate it repeatedly for its fidelity to Scripture and sensitivity to the Spirit in its application. Never do we want to wander from His standard or His side.

The Word Beyond the Church Doors

The Spirit's promise to accompany and empower His Word does not apply exclusively within the church doors. Just as it would be ludicrous to sheathe the sword of the Spirit if we were looking to grow spiritually, either as an individual believer or as a congregation, so also it would be a mistake to expect the Spirit to work apart from the Word in the world outside the church.

When Paul calls upon us to take up the sword of the Spirit, which is the Word of God, it is for the purpose of standing against the devil's schemes. "For our struggle is not against flesh and blood, but against the rulers, against the authorities, against the powers of this dark world and against the spiritual forces of evil in the heavenly realms" (Eph. 5:11–12). This includes the devil's schemes in our own lives; it also includes the prevailing ideas of our society. Scripture addresses societal issues and philosophical commitments. The Spirit calls upon us to bring Scripture to bear on these larger issues.

Philosophical viewpoints of recent centuries have all left their mark on the outlook of people in our times. Enlightenment rationalism, romanticism, pragmatism, existentialism, and now postmodernism have shaped our culture's commitments. For example, we can still see the effects of the Enlightenment's claim that human ability furnishes the resource by which culture becomes better and better. This is the American way! It suggests that the greatest thing we can do for everyone is educate them. But this fails to take into account the perversion of the human heart and the brokenness of life after the Fall.

Postmodernism, to take another example, claims that it is no longer possible to think that a single interpretation of life is true. Instead, various ideas about what is true are simply cultural constructions.[1] Postmodernism would have us believe that there is no longer any possibility of objective knowledge; rather, we create reality ourselves. Scripture directly challenges this privatization of truth. The gospel is the good news of salvation; that includes good news concerning the possibility of truth.

The church continually faces the challenge of making its message clear to the culture around it without diluting that message in word or action. At no time may we resort to human constructs to the exclusion of God's Word. Sometimes we feel that unbelievers' ideas and commitments are so far afield from God's truth that the words of Scripture would be incomprehensible or repulsive to them. But we must resist the pressure to omit the very words of God in our communication.

Why? Because Scripture alone is the authorized word, the official interpretation of reality, the certified self-revelation of God. It is the text that the Spirit promises to accompany with power and always with spiritual effect.

Paul set an important example in this regard in his address to the philosophers in Athens (Acts 17:16–34). In the Areopagus, that virtual cradle of Western civilization, where "all the Athenians and the foreigners who lived there spent their time doing nothing but talking about and listening to the latest ideas" (v. 21), Paul was asked to explain the new teaching he was presenting. He demonstrated that he understood their thinking. In their many attempts at religion, including even an altar to an unknown God, Paul perceived their religious desire and presented the good news of Christ as the answer to their search.

It did not matter that the Athenians were not well versed in Scripture or even in a Jewish cultural orientation. Paul still used the sword of the Spirit directly. He referred to Genesis to teach that God is the Creator, and to Isaiah 42:5 to declare that God is the source of life. He referred to Genesis 11:8 and Deuteronomy 32:8 to teach that God is sovereign over men and nations throughout history. Using Jeremiah 10:23 and Daniel 5:23, Paul taught that God holds everything about man in His own hand.

He pointed to the Resurrection as an undeniable fact of history to justify his claim that Christ will judge all men. Paul addressed the philosophy of his day with the Word of God.

Yes, it is important to understand what culture is saying, what our neighbor is saying. If we do not understand the issues, we cannot correctly apply God's Word in a way that will be understood. Also, if we do not recognize the impact of cultural ideas, we may not perceive the extent to which those ideas have subtly skewed our own interpretation of the Bible. We cannot simply expect to quote Scripture without doing our homework to insure the aptness and comprehensibility of our application of it. Do the homework; strive to understand the situation to which the Word must now be applied. And having done that, do apply the Word. Unsheathe the sword of the Spirit. Speak to the situation with the authoritative Word of God.

Our church must use the Word of God faithfully. We must make sure it has priority in our teaching, and that we depend continually on the Holy Spirit to illuminate us and cause us to grow. We must see that we are faithfully applying it in our individual lives. We must strive to apply it as we develop and fulfill church ministries. We must use it as we address the world in which God has placed us.

In doing this, our church conforms to God's pattern for health. The church that faithfully uses God's Word in continual dependence on the Holy Spirit remains tapped in to the sole source of divine power for spiritual change.

Elders Take the Lead

Suppose that you, with God's enabling, now recognize that in your church something reigns which is not the Bible. What will turn this around?

The change must be worked by the Spirit in and through the church's elders. No movement, no matter how biblical, which remains lay, will transform a church. No change can be significantly effected unless the church's official leadership commits itself to that change.

If you are an elder, what did you think you were doing when you took your ordination vows? What did you mean when you subscribed to Scripture, when you committed yourself to the inerrancy of the Word? Some elders need to wake up and seriously consider the implications of their formal commitment to its authority. How do you demonstrate submission to it? How should your leadership in this area play out in church life and ministry? Do not the elders' formal vows imply that the Bible should be held up as the unchallenged hallmark in their church?

Several upcoming chapters address the critical role of the elder within a church body. At this point, let me simply make the association for you; keep it in mind as you move on through this book.

Questions for Discussion

1. In your church, what commitments exist which threaten to usurp the authority intended for the Bible alone? Consider these possible usurpers, or add your own to the list:
   - a theological system
   - a theological doctrine
   - a style of worship
   - a certain person's teaching

- a code of behavior
- a social or ethnic criterion
- a philosophy of church growth
- a particular ministry
- a political agenda
- other: _____

2. Having isolated your church's potential usurpers, what evidence can you provide that the Bible remains more important than any of these, or that one of these has for now taken charge?

3. What areas in particular need to be addressed that we have discussed in this chapter?

4. How do your elders and their leadership figure into the role that the Bible or usurpers play in your church?

Chapter 4 Divine Motivation for Spiritual Life and Ministry

> **Healthy Practice #2:** The church must engage in regular vibrant worship to God as the ultimate motivation for personal and corporate growth.

It can't be assumed that every member wants to be a vital part of his or her church, that the people in the church want to continue together through thick and thin, or that a church will be willing to do what it takes to be healthy. It's not every group of people that becomes a vibrant church organism, strong, unified, and resilient through many circumstances and challenges. Being a church is about becoming, growing, moving, and pursuing something beyond the tangibles and beyond where we are now. It calls for ongoing change. We as a church are a composite of all the decisions we make, as we'll see. We are a group pursuing and implementing a vision, we'll also see. Health, we agreed, is moving toward Christlikeness, both as individuals and as a group. Leadership, we'll see, involves "moving and shaking"—provoking people to be dissatisfied with the status quo and inducing them to pursue change.

Where there needs to be change, there will have to be motivation to change. What will it take to make us want to change and grow, and to keep at it not just for this week or month or year or period in life, but for an entire lifetime? Where the most important reality is intangible, as it is in the church, it is a mistake to think that change and growth will be attained automatically, without determined effort. What will motivate us to pursue this goal?

One of life's big motivators is money. We do all kinds of things that we wouldn't do if someone weren't paying us to do it. But the church consists almost entirely of volunteers, and paid staff can receive an income low enough to need to be "not in it for the money." Obviously, our motivation must be something other than money.

But other motives are not necessarily biblical. We can often be induced to do something for the wrong reasons: self-aggrandizement, personal peace and prosperity, guilt, threats, preserving appearances. For a church to be biblically healthy, it must be motivated to change for the right reasons. Does the Bible indicate how God motivates us?

Presumably not every motive would be strong enough to motivate a group to pursue a lifelong task. Church health and personal involvement in a local church are lifelong tasks. But let's look at other lifelong tasks, such as marriage, parenting, and vocation. These responsibilities can be carried out successfully only if they are motivated by love—steadfast love. But love of what or whom? Not love of self, and sometimes not even love of the person or object involved. Christians know that it is our love for God, and, even more basically, His unconditional love for us, that motivates faithful, healthy service and growth.

Of course, this motivation pertains to church life and ministry. The best, most effective of all motivations, which is larger than all of life, is meeting, knowing, loving, and being loved by the living Lord.

For a church to be healthy, it must tap into this source of motivation. It must resist all attempts to veil it or replace it. It must not settle for the expedient motivation or even a good motivation in place of the best. The church which successfully "catches the wave" of vital love for and by God will know His richest blessing. "Draw near to God, and He will draw near to you" (James 4:8 NASB).

I am often asked, when I am teaching people about church health, if love shouldn't be listed as one of the key characteristics or evidences of a healthy church. Love is, indeed, the ultimate evidence of health, in both the life of the individual Christian and the body life of the church. At the heart of Christianity are the continually growing wonder at God's sovereign love, the loving response of worship and obedience, and the love of brothers and sisters in Christ for each other. Let me quote a marvelous Scripture passage that you may already be thinking of in this connection:

> Dear friends, let us love one another, for love comes from God. Everyone who loves has been born of God and knows God. Whoever does not love does not know God, because God is love. This is how God showed his love among us: He sent his one and only Son into the world that we might live through him. This is love: not that we loved God, but that he loved us and sent his Son as an atoning sacrifice for our sins. Dear friends, since God so loved us, we also ought to love one another. No one has ever seen God; but if we love one another, God lives in us and his love is made complete in us. (1 John 4:7–12)

It is certainly the case that a church evidencing these characteristics is evidencing health. In a way, this active, three-dimensional love can be seen as both the motive and the result of all the practices of a healthy church. But this does not mean that we no longer need to specify these practices. It is wonderful to talk about love, but sometimes, in talking about love, we can neglect to examine concretely how we are expressing it or how we're failing to express it. Yes, we should all love each other; but if that is not happening, simply declaring that we ought to be doing it will not fix the problem. Sometimes a congregation may experience a temporary euphoria that they identify as love, but because it has no foundation of the sort we discuss in this book, the honeymoon, as we say, is soon over. Perhaps we can consider our examination of these concrete practices of a healthy church as a scrutinizing of the anatomy of love. I believe that practicing health will result in a lifelong love, not merely a temporary euphoria.

I might have called this chapter "Love and Its Healthy Practice," for God's love for us is indeed the divine motivation for all spiritual life and ministry. Instead, I have chosen to identify this healthy practice as worship. This is because worship is the concrete activity that we can and must practice well in order to maintain our awareness of God's sovereign love, and in order to maintain His love as our primary motivation for ongoing spiritual growth.

As I have studied God's Word and assessed church life, I have concluded that vital corporate worship holds the primary key to motivation through the love of God. Fellowship and personal spiritual fulfillment offer important secondary sources of motivation. There are many short-term motivators as well. Let's explore all of these, moving from proximate to ultimate motives. We'll see that motivations other than love of God only "work" if they tap into that primary source; apart from it, they are useless over the long haul.

I've seen churches that lack this ultimate motivation, and I've seen churches that have it. The ones that lack it lack the "glue" to hold them together through difficult times. The ones who have it stick together and grow against all odds, in a way that can't be explained in terms of particular factors. The churches that are actively motivated by the love of God find it relatively easy to get people involved in their life and ministry. The ones for whom this motivation is not foremost find it relatively difficult to involve members in service.

I remember a church that was rebuilding after a fire had completely destroyed their facilities. It was easy to see that the congregation was highly involved in the church's ministry. I pondered what it was that was working so well. The actual rebuilding program could have been (and was) motivating people, but I sensed a deeper dynamic as well.

In the first two or three weeks after the fire, there was an enthusiastic outpouring of faith that God would now do even greater things than before. But that was followed by several difficult months of soul-searching. Differences of opinion concerning the direction of the church, differences that had existed before the fire, were now openly expressed. But in answer to much heart-wrenching prayer, the Lord granted the whole church an awareness of unrestricted, open joy in its worship experiences. This in turn brought a sense of His leading in this new opportunity to serve the Lord. The church came alive; everyone displayed enthusiasm and willingness to do whatever it took to accomplish God's purpose.

Ostensibly, the building program motivated them. In reality, it was part of something bigger: they were being drawn by their renewal in vital worship to a spiritual commitment to use the building program to actualize a unique opportunity to serve the Lord.

The healthy church is the one that is regularly meeting God and responding actively to Him.

Events and Activities

Many church events serve to energize involvement. We need to see these as legitimate, but short-term motivators. Special services at Christmas and Easter, the occasional guest speaker, family life conferences, covered-dish suppers, and building programs all offer an explicit goal that encourages people to achieve it, while fostering unity and spiritual growth in the quest. However, these things do not produce the kind of motivation needed for the long haul. Nobody participating seriously in church life would say that they do so simply because of these activities. As we shall see presently, short-term motivators do contain elements of a deeper, more satisfying dynamic.

Some programs and activities offer a degree of sustained motivation. Vital youth groups, neighborhood Bible studies, Sunday school, and outstanding church music are typical examples. Yes, we should encourage these activities and avail ourselves of the motivational momentum they furnish. But even these, in and of themselves, never substitute for the deeper motivation God uses to bond people into a living organism (1 Cor. 12:24) that can weather difficulties and disagreements as well as enjoy successes.

Deeper Dynamics: Fellowship and Fulfillment

All of the sources of motivation that we've mentioned, both short- and long-term, tap into two deeper dynamics: fellowship and fulfillment. This should not come as any surprise. We don't go to church looking for activities and accomplishments; we participate in the activities and projects because through them we enjoy something deeper.

Many church members cite fellowship when asked about their church's greatest strength. We love the universal "neighborly greeting and gossip" time before each service, social activities after almost every church function, families of the church getting together for picnics, trips, etc. Such light fellowship is indeed a blessing and should be sought. Sometimes we mistakenly believe that this is all the church really is, and that therefore everything that the church engages in must enable such fellowship.

The greatest benefit of light fellowship is that it creates the opportunity for the Holy Spirit to develop deeper, spiritual bonds within the body. The word *fellowship,* a translation of the Greek word *koinonia,* carries with it at least four concepts: deep, fulfilling relationships (1 John 1:3), a unified body of people (1 Cor. 1:9), communication (Gal. 6:6), and communion (1 Cor. 10:16).

We have only to ponder the Lord's Supper to glimpse the nature of true fellowship. The apostle Paul says:

> Is not the cup of thanksgiving for which we give thanks a participation in the blood of Christ? And is not the bread that we break a participation in the body of Christ? Because there is one loaf, we, who are many, are one body, for we all partake of the one loaf. (1 Cor. 10:16–17)

Every time we take the Lord's Supper we are compelled to ask afresh, "What made it worthwhile for Christ to die for me? Why did He do it?" Communion makes us wrestle with what motivated Jesus. Looking deeper into my own heart, I cry out that there is nothing in me worthy of Christ's dying for me. This causes me to marvel again at the love and grace that God gave me when He brought Christ to the cross. Over and over again I am compelled to conclude that He wanted to die simply because of His perfect, infinite love for me.

This renewed, deepened sense of comprehension of Christ's motivation for dying comes by my participating—"fellowshipping," if you will, for *koinonia* is the word used for *participating*—in His body and blood, by faith. And my increased sensitivity to His motivation in turn motivates me. It is not merely that I am blessed. It motivates me to become part of deeper relationships within the church. I find that I am not satisfied until I share (participate) with another member or other members deeply enough to know them well and have them know me, to anticipate their needs and problems, practice tolerance, and offer support and love. These key ingredients knit members into a deeply unified body and motivate the group for life and ministry. Fellowship is experiencing the body of the living Christ.

A second dynamic strongly motivates us to active life and ministry, and that is spiritual fulfillment. Ultimately, spiritual fulfillment is participation, actively and passively, in the kingdom of God. It consists of seeing that God is at work, both passively, in my own life, and actively, through me in the lives of others. We experience fulfillment when we see that the things happening to us and the things we do make a difference for the kingdom.

Just as with fellowship, we sometimes limit our concept of fulfillment to things that are good, but superficial. We teach a Sunday school class or bake cookies for a reception. We think that these things make us feel useful. Leadership can promote this superficial approach: if certain people in the congregation do not yet hold down some post at church, we think we have to keep at them until they do. Sometimes we measure our growth in terms of what we learn. Woe to the pastor from whom we learn nothing new in four weeks! We tend to think and speak of fulfillment in such terms because we can measure them more easily than we can the deeper dynamics.

In reality, we feel that we are participating actively in the kingdom of God when we see that He is using us to serve others in the name of Christ. We sense that we have done something significant that He is using, to which He replies, "Well done!" He allows us to hear that others benefit from this ministry. This experience builds a godly, biblical self-confidence: God is using the gifts and graces with which the Spirit has equipped me. The more we serve, the bolder we become in service. It brings tremendous freedom in ministry, along with this sense of fulfillment.

Passively, we experience spiritual fulfillment as we sense that God is causing us to grow, ministering to us through others, through our quiet times of devotion, and through church activities. We know the joy of being conformed to Christ, so that we more readily discern His will and obey it cheerfully, recognizing that His design represents what is best for us. We wrestle with the questions of life and find in our God the only—and the perfect—answer. We grow in our understanding of who He is, especially in corporate worship, as we listen to the Word expounded, as we pray and sing His praises together, as we confess our sins and together give ourselves to Him.

Active and passive spiritual fulfillment complement and supplement one another. They know no limit; they are as infinite as God Himself. Together they motivate us powerfully to move "further up and further in."[1] They stimulate our church's cohesiveness and drive to accomplish God's will.

In my first solo pastorate, I came to know the deep motivation that a sense of fulfillment brings. For the first four and a half years, the church evidenced no growth—no motion toward spiritual maturity and no addition of members beyond our thirty-three or so. We even bought land and built a building, but no spiritual vitality resulted.

So I met with each of the elders. One by one, they confronted me seriously about my ministry. Interaction was tense, but we ended each time with intense prayer. I was learning humility, and so were they.

In the next year and a half, we saw many people come to Christ as Savior. The church grew to over a hundred. The level of fellowship was deepening all the time, and the power of the Lord's presence in the Lord's Supper was unmistakable. I gained a sense of fulfillment as I saw God working in me and through me. I gained a growing awareness of the confidence and freedom that we can have in ministry when we see God using us.

Fellowship and fulfillment, understood and experienced deeply, motivate believers as individuals and as a body to long-lasting, active commitment to Christ and to each other, to personal and corporate Christlikeness. But I believe that fellowship and fulfillment, important and essential as they are, represent secondary motivational dynamics. A deeper level remains for us to explore.

The Primary Motivator: Vital Worship

The key element in both fulfillment and fellowship is God at work. God is binding us together in unity and love; God is using us in each other's lives. But, to put it baldly, neither of these things would mean much to us if God Himself were not important to us! God is binding us together? So what? God is using us? Who's He? If we suffer from a paltry view of God, any significance remaining in fellowship or fulfillment will be, to that degree, merely human.

This leads me to claim that the primary motivator for involvement in church life and ministry is regular, corporate, vital worship, for here we encounter the living God. To know God is to be changed radically. It always implies action; a person cannot be said to know God without responding to Him. This encounter is and always must be what motivates anything—what motivates everything. Should any other motivator conflict with this, we would be idolaters.

And if this encounter is so critical, is it not incumbent upon churches to make vital worship a reality? Could it not be said to be our primary responsibility?[2] To block or veil vital worship, intentionally or unintentionally, is a serious mistake that has far-reaching implications.

The Key Ingredient: Spiritual Thirst

What makes worship vital? If worship follows the pattern of fellowship and fulfillment, it will be easier to measure worship in terms of tangible items, such as music or preaching, but these may not represent the heart of the matter.

Perhaps we can best express the essence of worship by saying that it is a deep-seated longing, a thirsting for God that is satisfied as He reveals Himself to us. Worship thus contains two basic elements: the soul's thirst for God and God's self-revelation. As we examine them, we get a better idea of how God means to motivate us for life and ministry.

Psalm 42:1–3 articulates the believer's longing for God:

> As the deer pants for streams of water,
> so my soul pants for you, O God.

My soul thirsts for God, for the living God.
When can I go and meet with God?
My tears have been my food day and night,
while men say to me all day long, "Where is
your God?"

Anyone this desperate to be with God would seek Him with undying energy. Anyone with this spiritual thirst would long to worship in His presence. Anyone with this degree of thirst would derive profound satisfaction from the experience of worship.

Brothers and sisters, this is most often the missing dimension we need to be the kind of worshipers God seeks (John 4:23), and for our worship to be vital. Many, if not most, Christians enjoy being in church, but at the same time they do not really thirst for God. They don't experience this thirst in their daily lives, and so they do not bring it to corporate worship. They do not see corporate worship as the apex of a life of walking in worship with their God. Yes, they come anticipating fellowship, teaching, and fulfillment. They anticipate the time-honored patterns of the service. They even come willing to be challenged to apply the Word to their lives, and to look for the Spirit to change them.

But in all these worthy elements the goal is to meet personal needs and desires. Spiritual thirst is simply the longing to meet and know God Himself. When the twenty-four elders of Revelation 4 meet the living God, they "fall down before him who sits on the throne, and worship him who lives for ever and ever," and they lay their crowns before Him (v. 10). The Greeks told the disciples simply this: "Sir, we would like to see Jesus" (John 12:21). Mary simply sat at His feet, earning the Savior's commendation that she had "chosen what is better, and it will not be taken away from her" (Luke 10:42). Moses, who needed

God to help him accomplish many impossible tasks, asked God also for the ultimate blessing: "Now show me your glory" (Ex. 33:18). Whatever we expect God to do for us, and whatever we expect to do for Him—and these are legitimate, praiseworthy expectations—the greater expectation, the greater desire that He can and will fulfill, is simply the desire to meet Him. This longing and its fulfillment are the deepest of all. Augustine prayed, "You have made us for yourself, and our heart is restless until it rests in you."[3]

Does my soul exhibit this spiritual thirst? Does yours? If not, how is it to be obtained? It cannot be acquired magically or overnight! Perhaps it begins with longing for the longing. Think of it as something that we cultivate and that God works in us. (Would this not also describe human love?)

Longing for God grows out of knowing two things—and perhaps a third: (1) who He is, (2) who we are, and (3) that the one corresponds perfectly to the other. John Calvin begins his *Institutes of the Christian Religion* by puzzling over which kind of knowledge comes first: knowledge of God or knowledge of self. He concludes that we simply can't have one without the other: to know God is to see ourselves accurately; to know ourselves is to see our need of God. As we come to the Lord regularly in private devotions, we must seek to learn about Him and about ourselves and expect to find that He offers everything that we need. We can cultivate this as a way of life that extends well beyond our quiet times to include every hour of every day. The more we know these things, the more we long to meet God. Eternity will not be long enough to plumb the depths of God; worship will go on eternally. Our spiritual thirst will never be eradicated, and it will always be satisfied.

Compare this with a person falling in love. I talk about "getting to know her"—I don't seem to tire of it, or to think that I will ever exhaust the possibilities. I compare her to myself: we have so much in common, as well as wonderful differences. The bottom line is that I long for more; I'm happy only in the pursuit.

Vital corporate worship, in addition to being fueled by vital private worship, should fuel private worship in turn. As long as we do not bar the public from our services and in fact seek to bring them in, we can expect that some people will experience their first tantalizing exposure to God in corporate worship. We find ourselves surrounded by all kinds of different people, indicating the breadth of God's grace in reaching out to mankind. We experience its power to unify us as we break bread together in communion. We know the joy and security of belonging, which flows from fellowship with the saints. We experience divine nourishment in the sacraments. We see God revealed powerfully in the preaching of the Word. Our hearts thrill as we sing praises to His name. We cry out to Him together in prayer and sense His presence in the group (Matt. 18:20). We grow in seeing how precious Jesus is. Corporate worship thus makes us thirsty even as it quenches that thirst.

But that thirst must be quenched. Thirst by itself could never be satisfying! Our longing must be met by the reality of that for which we long. We must meet God, and we must meet Him in His fullness.

And do I need to say it? How do we find out about God? He reveals Himself to us in the Bible. That is why we read it daily, and that explains the centrality of the sermon in corporate worship. The mere reading or hearing of the Bible will not do. The believer must appropriate what he or she hears.

The believer successfully appropriates the Word to the extent that he or she perceives God's character to be like his or her own. God created us in His image, Genesis 1 and 2 tell us.

By creating us in His image, God imaged Himself in us. Like responds to like. Therefore, as we perceive the various facets of God's character during the worship service, the corresponding facets in us expand and respond with excitement. His image in us offers a natural conduit to vitalize our submission and adoration. It is the way we know that we have met with the living God in worship and grow in Him through worship.

God is intelligent; we also have minds. He is moral; we have a conscience. He evidences feelings; we have emotions. He demonstrates volition; so do we. He is holy; we are aware of holiness. He is the essence of beauty; we appreciate beauty. He is a communicator; we also have the ability to communicate with God through prayer. He is active in creation and providence; He has created in us the drive to work and has called us to it.

For a worship service to be vital, all these facets of our and God's nature must be easily discernible. We must see God's intelligence and His feelings, His holiness and His beauty. Our own intelligence and emotions, our sense of holiness and of beauty must be engaged or addressed. We come to know Him in His multifaceted character, and we come to know ourselves in the process. We see the similarity; we see the difference. We see Him, and we respond to Him in adoration and submission. And He changes us radically.

In terms of this model, we can easily see how a truncated worship experience can lead to aberrations of faith and practice. For instance, if corporate worship emphasizes emotions, the church begins to look for physical manifestations of God's work during its services in order to verify that He is blessing us. If the church emphasizes the intellectual aspect, the power of the Spirit becomes overshadowed by the prowess of human logic. Services can become lectures surrounded by archaic formality. If a church dwells exclusively on active response, it may miss the message of God's sovereign grace. If none of the facets of God's character are evident in the service, the church soon becomes a dead organization, bound together only by human loyalties and/or financial obligations.

For a worship service to have vital worship, at least three things are required. First and most obviously, the Spirit must be working in and through the people of the church. Second, a preacher is needed who combines meaningful, biblical scholarship, comprehension of the dynamics driving today's culture, and pastoral insight about contemporary living. The Word must be persuasively proclaimed and insightfully applied. Third, the service must be geared to achieving vital worship of the living God.

About this last feature, much can be said. And we can never expect to close the book on the subject, for it will develop as the church's cultural and temporal context changes. But the worship experience is considerably strengthened when the congregation recognizes that the pastor is himself worshiping, and not simply conducting the service. Learning to worship is like learning any skill: we need to see how it's done. It's never enough simply to be told to do it!

A Few Examples

When I think about what God can accomplish through us in regular corporate worship, different examples come to mind. I will share them with you to prompt your own analysis of your church's practice: Does it successfully offer worshipers a vital encounter with the living God? Does it display God's character in its multifaceted richness, enabling worshipers to respond to Him from the many facets of their own likeness to Him? Or is one facet emphasized in such a way as to overshadow the others? Are all possible distractions removed that might bridle the joyous and unqualified proclamation of the Word or its reception by the hearers? Are we mistakenly focusing on, rigid about, or quibbling over styles of worship in such a way as to hinder believers from cultivating and satisfying their longing for God?

Let me start with my recollection of an outstanding corporate worship experience that I enjoyed with a church that was meeting in, yes, a bakery! "The only bread we offer is the Bread of Life!" was their motto, and they truly "delivered"! The church's leaders evidenced a complete commitment to the Word and to the Lord. You could tell that there was no reservation in their hearts: they opened themselves to God and to the people, and they spoke the Word with authority. Corporate worship included all the biblically specified elements of worship, and it addressed all aspects of God's character. The church had done what it could to make the worship experience accessible to all with a minimum of distractions. The end result was that you forgot that you were in a bakery shop, because you experienced in a compelling way the presence and majesty of the living God.

Beautiful facilities do enhance our worship, but we should never deem them either necessary or sufficient. The key ingredient of vital worship lies elsewhere: the cultivation and satisfying of spiritual thirst.

The wrong ingredient. Some churches overemphasize a different ingredient, and in doing this they deny their congregation the richness that should attend an encounter with the living God. In some churches the liturgy or the order of worship has stopped being a tool to assist this encounter and has come to be prized as the essence of what the church gathers to do.

Can you picture a carpenter loving his hammer so much that he talks to it or takes it out to dinner? How silly! Similarly, we should focus not on the particular procedures, but on the living God. The procedures are tools, means to the end. To focus on them eclipses the reality they were shaped to serve. To focus on them introduces an unbiblical element; we experience the kind of rigidity and sterility that results from adding to the Word of God.

I once worshiped with a small African-American church. During that service, everyone present came forward to put their offering into the plate. Then, also during the service, that collection was counted and the total announced. If the amount was deemed inadequate, they kept going—more and more money was solicited. It became apparent that the congregation's sense of the presence and power of the Lord in worship was tied to the amount of offering that they, under the ongoing prompting of the leaders, were able to raise. They missed the presence and power of the Lord in many other aspects of His Word and of their lives.

I remember a chapel service in which a very emotional speaker led in prayer. In the course of that prayer, he knocked his glasses off the pulpit and stamped on them without ever noticing it! He seemed to believe that the power of God's presence was directly proportional to the amount of energy he expended in leading worship. In this instance, as in the previous ones, the overemphasized ingredient was not in itself evil; rather, the mistake lay in the overemphasis that excluded the real key to vital worship, namely, satisfying an ever-growing longing for the living God.

Overemphasizing Christian experience. Another problem occurs when too much emphasis is placed on the worshipers, eclipsing the Worshiped One. In one contemporary service I attended, I noticed that the traditional invocation had been replaced by a "preparation for worship." I sensed that the congregation was more concerned about themselves doing something for God, than their need for Him to do something for them. But no amount of personal preparation can ever substitute for the Lord's own presence and power among us! It's just like conversion: our personal choice of Christ is essential. But once we've become Christians, we understand that what is critical to our redemption is not our choice of Him so much as His sovereign choice of us. To allow the one to stand for the other would be a serious and deadly misrepresentation of the gospel.

The invocation summons the living God to meet with His gathered people. This is a formal, ceremonial pleading for almighty God to choose to be with us at this service. God is awesome, magnificent, and infinite, and here we sinners meet, saved by His grace. We do not deserve it, but we beg for His presence. Unless He graciously condescends to meet with us, nothing will distinguish this gathering from any other meeting. Without His presence, we cannot experience the vital worship and the motivation it affords our ongoing spiritual maturation.

Sometimes our choice of hymns and the way we testify to Christ focuses on the saved rather than the Savior. When I was a young man, my father, a man with no apparent interest in the Lord or the church, one time commented to me, "All I hear about in what you say and sing is what God does for *you.*" That was a wake-up call for me! In later years, with his criticism in mind, I scrutinized the hymns we had used. In that selection of songs there was only one hymn about God Himself or about the great truths of the Christian faith, and that was "Holy, Holy, Holy"; all the rest he had astutely pegged as being about the singers' Christian experience. Worship is lopsided if it focuses on me and my experience, not on the living God!

We focus inappropriately on believers rather than on their Christ when entertainment eclipses worship. I'll never forget one extreme example: one service I attended went on and on, with many special music numbers and testimonies. When the guest speaker was summoned to the pulpit, he turned to the congregation and said, believe it or not: "You're all too tired to hear anything—Amen!"

Inhibiting the proclamation of the Word. We must do everything we can to guarantee that the Word of God is proclaimed with God's own authority. I've noticed a potentially dangerous development in some contemporary worship services that strive to be seeker friendly. Speakers avoid saying, "Thus says the Lord." Listeners are offered reasoned support, but not authoritative support for what God calls us to do and be. Absent is any sense that God's revelation is being declared. Logic should confirm and commend the declaration of God's Word, but it should never replace it. God the Spirit indwells and works through His authoritative revelation. To replace proclamation entirely with persuasion or logic deprives hearers of the possibility of God's power in their lives.

Criticism can also inhibit preaching. If a pastor feels threatened by possible criticism from a segment of his congregation, his ministry of the Word will be hampered, and the presence and power of the living Lord will in that measure be restricted. I observed this in one church in which I sensed a certain degree of fear under the surface of the worship. As I discussed this with the pastor later, I learned that a third of his session espoused theonomy, an interpretation of the Old Testament with which he disagreed. Whenever he entered the pulpit, he feared their criticism: "They're going to tell me what I did wrong." He was exhibiting fear and restraint in conducting the service, and in that measure the powerful and active ministry of the Lord was obscured.

Of course, any church which fails to understand the authoritative role of the Word of God will to that extent limit His powerful action in believers' hearts. To relate an extreme example: I visited one church—not one that I would call "evangelical"—in which the sermon was replaced by a series of billboards surrounding the congregation. Members were asked to circulate around to all the billboards, stopping at one that especially appealed to them. Then they were to share their ideas with the other people who gathered at that billboard. Social consciousness or personal awareness had entirely replaced the declaration of the revelation of the living, majestic, transcendent God.

Handling the distractions. In order to offer worshipers a vital encounter with the Lord, leaders must do what they can to minimize potential distractions, so that the worshipers can focus without undue difficulty on that encounter. This involves taking steps ahead of time and preparing helpers for possible eventualities. It's important to make attenders as comfortable as possible. This includes everything from setting the thermostat to having a competent nursery staff.

It makes good sense for the pastor and worship leaders to meet with, not the elders, but the deacons and ushers, prior to each service. I say this because the deacons will be involved in caring for comfort and addressing distractions during the service. They should be clued in on what will be happening, and everyone will benefit from their joining in prayer for God's hand on all these matters. Anyone who has been involved in leading worship knows well the many things that can and do go wrong on Sunday morning. It is not unbiblical to expect that Satan will operate his own business of sabotage, precisely because he understands how God works and means to thwart it. What better response is there than to engage the support team with you in prayer? And why not pray with the elders? Before the service, they should be engaged in their primary activity, which, as we shall see, is shepherding. They should be greeting people.

The goal of worship is to enable the congregation to meet with the living Lord. We must strive to focus our efforts on that key ingredient, cultivating and satisfying the longing of the human heart for God. For this to occur, all biblical elements of worship—the call to worship, prayer, singing praise, confession of sin, preaching, and the sacraments—must be present. Extraneous elements must be reduced as much as possible. God must be represented in all of His facets, answering to the corresponding dimensions of His image bearers. And the whole service must demonstrate the joy and celebration of leaders and worshipers giving their hearts to the Lord and His Word.

God Has Always Motivated Action Through Worship

Throughout human history, God has used worship, an encounter with Himself, to motivate action as well as to glorify His name. The prophet Isaiah's experience (Isa. 6:1–8) is paradigmatic. He had a vision of the Lord "seated on a throne, high and exalted, and the train of his robe filled the temple." He saw God surrounded by angels who demonstrated and spoke of God's holiness, shaking the temple and filling it with smoke.

"Woe to me!" Isaiah cried. "I am ruined! For I am a man of unclean lips, and I live among a people of unclean lips, and my eyes have seen the King, the LORD Almighty!" He recognized that he had to die because of his sinfulness in the presence of the holy God.

But God exercised His grace, healing him at the point of his need. With a burning coal, He cleansed Isaiah's unclean lips.

Then God summoned him to serve: "Whom shall I send? And who will go for us?"

Put yourself in Isaiah's sandals in the awesome terror of that moment: you have been face-to-face with the living God. You have seen that you have no right to continue living beyond this experience. But you have experienced God's unqualified forgiveness. You are *His.* Would you not do anything He called you to do?

Isaiah's classic response was "Here am I. Send me!" Meeting the living God led to Isaiah's joyful submission to His will. Worship motivated him to action on a level that no other force could approximate.

Moses met the living God at the burning bush (Ex. 3). He saw God control nature itself. He witnessed God's gracious response to his own fears. God revealed to Moses His own name, "I am who I am." Moses then embarked on a humanly impossible task. His experience of worship motivated him.

Peter and John were dragged to prison, severely threatened, and then released. They returned to the believers, told their story, and participated in a corporate prayer meeting. After praising God gloriously, they prayed: "Now, Lord, consider their threats and enable your servants to speak your word with great boldness" (Acts 4:29). In the context of worship, God motivated the entire group to stand for Him.

We can see this pattern in the life and ministry of the New Testament church. Paul described the Thessalonians' conversion, that they "turned to God from idols to serve the living and true God" (1 Thess. 1:9). God had graciously granted the Thessalonians rebirth. They responded by worshiping Him and then began to serve Him, openly waiting for His return.

Each time we worship the living God, He thrills our hearts as we recall His gift of love—that He paid for our salvation by sacrificing Jesus. In vital worship, He overwhelms us with His infinite love. The church is the bride of Christ; we can expect our worship services to be like a wedding, a festival of joy and love as bride and bridegroom meet. The happy delight in their faces declares, "Believe it or not: I belong to Him and He belongs to me!" We know God's love afresh in corporate worship. We tap into the ultimate motive: God's sovereign love. Our only possible response is to follow in the Thessalonians' path and serve Him.

Compare one church, in which worship motivates more profoundly than fellowship, with another church, in which the two are reversed. When worship motivates, a congregation will also experience deep fellowship as they commit themselves together to follow Jesus at all costs. "Let us fix our eyes on Jesus, the author and perfecter of our faith, who for the joy set before him endured the cross, scorning its shame, and sat down at the right hand of the throne of God" (Heb. 12:2).

By contrast, a congregation motivated primarily by fellowship will in its life and ministry choose alternatives that enhance or protect human relationships. Worship may be relegated to second place. For example, the church may schedule services to fit the convenience of the general public. It may avoid church discipline, lest it threaten fellowship. It may avoid taking a stand on difficult doctrines or against society's injustices. The presence of church cliques (consisting of those in the fellowshipping group) may make visiting unbelievers uncomfortable.

We need proper biblical motivation to produce balanced biblical action. Skew the motive, and the action will evidence a corresponding distortion. Worship that is vital encounter with the living Lord, whose sovereign love drew us to Himself and holds us steadfastly in His care, the Lord for whom we thirst and who alone quenches that thirst, properly motivates individuals and the church body to faithful and delighted service. The healthy church employs this greatest of all motivations.

Questions for Discussion

Assess your church using these questions:

1. Does it successfully offer worshipers a vital encounter with the living God?
2. Does it display God's character in its multifaceted richness, enabling worshipers to respond to God from the many facets of their own likeness to Him?
3. Is one facet of worship emphasized in such a way as to overshadow the rest?
4. Are all distractions removed that might bridle the joyous and unqualified proclamation of the Word or its reception by the hearers?
5. Are we mistakenly focusing on, rigid about, or quibbling over concrete styles of worship in such a way as to obscure worship's primary ingredient: cultivating and satisfying believers' longing for God?

Part II

A Strategy for Healthy, Biblical Leadership

Chapter 5 Biblical Directives That Shape Church Life

For a church to be healthy, it needs healthy leadership. In my experience, leadership is one of only a few keys to being a church that God blesses. That is why I dedicate this book in large measure to church leaders, and why, in my consulting business, I work directly with them.

But what counts as "good leadership"? Is there a kind of leading that conforms to the Bible's vision of a healthy church (as over against a kind of leading that does not)? If the answer is yes, what would that healthy leadership look like? How would we know if our church has it, and what would we do if it doesn't?

Emphatically, yes: there is a kind of leading that both conforms to Scripture and increases church health. When it comes to church health, not just any old leadership will do. We must be careful to think through and implement concrete strategies of the sort I will suggest in these chapters.

In this chapter, we'll examine what the Bible says about church life and what it implies for church leadership. Chapters 6 and 7 discuss God's design for elders; as you'll see, design is best summed up by the word *shepherd*. In Chapter 8, I'll show you a concrete mechanism that enables a church to fulfill Scripture's ideals for church life and for shepherd ministry.

Biblical Directive #1: Treat Individual Members' Gifts with Integrity

Years of pastoring drove me continually to the Word to search for God's vision of His church, His blueprint for His temple, His dress for His bride. I longed to know this because it would show me what He wanted me, a pastor, to do and be. My job was to strive to shape His church to match His vision. Later, as my calling shifted to overseeing church-planting ministries, I still pursued this vision, so that I could help other pastors and churches understand God's plan.

I began to realize that the Bible gives two complementary directives that together imply a rather definite leadership structure. Apart from this leadership structure, it becomes well-nigh impossible to implement both of these complementary directives. Apart from it, one or the other of them must be sacrificed.

The first of those two biblical directives is that the church is a group of believers, each of whom should be exercising his or her gifts for the spiritual good of the group. "To each one the manifestation of the Spirit is given for the common good," Paul tells the Corinthian church (1 Cor. 12:7). He exhorts the Roman congregation: "We have different gifts, according to the grace given us. If a man's gift is prophesying, let him use it in proportion to his faith. If it is serving, let him serve; if it is teaching, let him teach; if it is encouraging, let him encourage; if it is contributing to the needs of others, let him give generously; if it is leadership, let him govern diligently; if it is showing mercy, let him do it cheerfully" (Rom. 12:6–8). The apostle Peter seconds the directive: "Each one should use whatever gift he has received to serve others, faithfully administering God's grace in its various forms" (1 Peter 4:10).

It couldn't be more clear: *each* member possesses a particular gift or aptitude that the Holy Spirit intends to bless as that member participates in church life. The church as a whole needs to *let* each one use his or her gift, and, in so doing, let the Holy Spirit do His work. God intends to use each one of us in each other's life and for the good of the whole.

God wants each one of us to take all individual gifts of the Spirit seriously. If God has given our member, John Smith, a gift of administration, He must think that our church needs John exercising that gift (note: not just the exercise of that gift, but John exercising that gift!). No gift is superfluous or redundant; every believer matters. This means that I need the ministry of yesterday's new member as much as he or she needs mine. "The eye cannot say to the hand, 'I don't need you!'" Paul says, comparing the human body to the body of Christ (1 Cor. 12:21).

This passage also contains deep comfort for the pastor and the core group of a struggling church or a church plant (a church just getting started): not only does every gift matter, but God has already given your church every gift, every person, that it needs for what He intends for you to do today and begin tomorrow! "But in fact God has arranged the parts in the body, every one of them, just as he wanted them to be" (v. 18). Impossible, you say? Yes, it is impossible, if your particular vision for your church dictates for all time the roles your members can play. But if we take God at His word, that He has in fact given us every gift we need, then our vision should be shaped by the people God has given at the present time, rather than the people being shaped by our vision. We'll talk more about this in part 3.

God wants us to treat other members' gifts with integrity. To do otherwise would be to shortchange the Spirit of God, to thwart His intentions. That can't be healthy! Taking believers' gifts seriously may well mean a shift in how churches do things. We'll see in part 3, as I've hinted, that it implies that people always take precedence over programs. We must continually reshape our programs in light of the ever-changing array of gifts that God gives our members.

The most fundamental implication of the biblical injunction to treat other members' gifts with integrity is this: biblical leadership must allow this to happen. Finding a way to do this is perhaps the hardest thing to do. The answer doesn't count as a quick fix! But it is perhaps the most critical need that a church has—the most significant key to church health. As I think over what I have to say in this book, it all blends together into a single picture. There are many strands woven through it. But if I had to single out one that undergirds every other, one without which the picture simply would not, could not, be what it is, it would be that leaders must treat individual members' gifts with integrity, even as they exercise accountability. When they do so, their church's health can be significantly enhanced.

Sad to say, my experience with churches in America leads me to believe that many leaders don't treat members' gifts with integrity. Indeed, many leaders don't even realize that they don't. In many churches with "strong leadership," the church's elders are perceived as a board of directors, as leaders who tell the people what to do. Such an attitude indicates to me that this church has failed to implement the Bible's commitment to the integrity of members' gifts.

I know of one large church that ordained and installed its elders for life. Of the church's fifty to sixty elders, more than half were well up in years and no longer able to participate actively. A small group of elders functioned like an executive committee, with the session as a whole only ratifying their decisions. From the congregation's point of view, this handful of elders carried out the work of the church.

We tend to label such leadership "strong leadership." But such leadership ignores the general membership when it comes to decision making. As a result, the people do not feel that their contribution is significant. Their spiritual gifts are not treated with integrity. Thus, the Holy Spirit is not honored, and the church cannot move forward in spiritual health!

If this is strong leadership, then we had better make a distinction. Perhaps it can be called strong leadership when a few people muscle their way into control (or gain control by default) and call all the shots. In a volunteer organization, such as a church, sometimes we're happy to let anybody work who is willing to work. But you can easily see, when we state it so baldly, that there must be a better type of leadership—stronger, perhaps, in a good sense, but not in the sense of being repressive, exclusive, or dictatorial. In the biblical model, as we'll see, elders must be liberating, enabling people in the congregation to be all that they can be. This approach takes even greater strength and more courage and trust. It takes loving involvement and lots of communication. It may seem to be more difficult, but it's what God calls us to do. We'll see in upcoming chapters how it can happen, what such mature leadership looks like.

Interestingly enough, the actual style of church leadership doesn't necessarily correspond to the church's formal polity. Every church has one of the three basic forms of government. A church has either a hierarchical (Episcopal), a republican (Presbyterian), or a congregational (Baptist/independent) form of government. You might expect that in congregational churches, members would most freely exercise their gifts. But all too often the members are locked into following the pastor, so that exercising their gifts does little to shape the church. In my own Presbyterian denomination, I find that a high percentage of our churches are, functionally speaking, hierarchical. The elected leaders make all the meaningful decisions; the congregation perceives them as a "corporate bishopric."

In fact, any denomination that takes seriously the Bible's summons to accountable leadership (the other directive, examined below) seems vulnerable to this misconception. Often people simply don't see how leadership can take a form that takes followers' contributions seriously.

Often a church exhibits a double imbalance. On the one hand, it views its elders as a board of directors, telling everybody what to do. On the other hand, incongruously, it believes that the congregation has a right to vote on everything—something near and dear to the hearts of Americans! In such a church, things move along as long as the leadership and the laity agree on how things should be done. However, if the leadership imposes a change, it may provoke the congregation, which believes it should have had a vote on the matter. One church I surveyed clearly exhibited these conflicting beliefs: 95 percent of the congregation believed that in their church the elders directed church affairs; 65 percent also indicated that church affairs were directed by congregational vote. But the biblical model of leadership is more than an uneasy tension between two mutually opposed, defective extremes. Biblical leadership should transform this working relationship in such a way that the two biblical directives are implemented harmoniously.

A church in which members' gifts are taken seriously is a church that honors the Holy Spirit's work in individuals, and one in which those individuals feel significant and valuable to

God's kingdom. It is no wonder that God intends for us to comply with this directive, for it glorifies Him expressly, advancing His kingdom in us and through us as it unleashes the Spirit's power. Our church's leadership must therefore treat individual spiritual gifts with integrity.

Biblical Directive #2: Regard Elders as Accountable to God

But now, treating members' gifts with integrity constitutes only half of the biblical picture. You can imagine the extreme: total member initiative without any kind of leadership results in chaos. Paul addressed a situation like this in the Corinthian church, reminding them that "God is not a God of disorder but of peace" (1 Cor. 14:33). God also exhorts us through Paul that the goal is not individual good, but the common good (1 Cor. 12:7). Rarely does a situation like this exist in an evangelical church today. Biblical leadership protects against it.

The Bible's other directive is this: regard a church's leaders as accountable to God for its members. "Obey your leaders and submit to their authority," the Hebrew Christians were told. "They keep watch over you as men who must give an account. Obey them so that their work will be a joy, not a burden, for that would be of no advantage to you" (Heb. 13:17). Paul speaks to Timothy of "the elders who direct the affairs of the church," indicating that some of them preach and teach and others do not (1 Tim. 5:17). The elders oversee the church's life and ministry in order to give an account to God of the people He has entrusted to their care.

Does this mean that the elders do all the work in the church? That would be impossible—although I have to say that I often see a harried, overworked leadership! Does it mean that the elders are supposed to tell everybody else what to do and how to do it? I believe that Scripture in no way supports that interpretation. While Scripture does expect elders to carry out certain responsibilities, there is no direct scriptural injunction regarding who should handle many matters that arise in a church. How a church handles them bears critically on the roles of the leadership and the membership.

If a church's leadership takes responsibility for everything, members' own contributions become comparatively insignificant. The members are turned into so many yes-men or worker bees. They perceive the elders as the only people who make decisions, as the directors whose instructions they carry out with little or no input in shaping them. In this situation, the Bible's other directive, to treat individual members' gifts with integrity, is no longer being actualized.

Balancing Accountable Leadership and Gift Integrity

But how can church leaders exercise accountability and at the same time treat members' gifts with integrity? The shepherd model of the elder (chapters 6 and 7) and the organizational mechanism that I propose (chapter 8) resolve this apparent conflict!

We begin to figure it out when we realize, as I said before, that not every decision must be made by the elders. Yes, God does relegate some decisions exclusively to them. For example, the elders must see to it that the Word of God is accurately and fully preached, that the sacraments are properly administered, and that discipline is properly maintained. Some other decisions belong exclusively to the congregation. For example, congregations call pastors, elect officers, and buy, develop, or sell land and facilities.

But when you stop to think about the choices that make our church's life and ministry what they are, most of them fall into neither of these categories. For example, should we emphasize day care, senior citizens' activities, or Christian education in order to meet our particular community's unique needs? Who will teach this Sunday school class? Will we plant peonies or barberries by the entrance? How can we encourage the young people to reach out to their friends at school? What do our women need most in the way of nurture? How will it be supplied?

The next step is to realize the difference between accountability and responsibility. To be responsible for something means that it is included in your job description. To be accountable means that God looks to you to see to it that it gets done, whether by you or by someone else. God holds elders accountable for all of their church's life and ministry, but this does not mean that they exercise responsibility for all of it. You can exercise accountability with respect to choices and ministries for which you are not responsible.

To state it positively, the elders must find a way to delegate to ordinary members the responsibility for key decisions in the life and ministry of the church, while at the same time maintaining accountability for the affairs of the church. The elders do not stand in place of the mix of spiritual gifts that God has assembled in a church. The elders lead and guide it, but God made the mix.

This hints at a leadership style that many of us experience in the working world. Some bosses specify every last thing that their employees are to do. For employees who don't want to think or be responsible, this is great; others who want to exercise initiative champ at the bit. Other bosses delegate huge portions of the company's activity to their employees, leaving room for them to influence the product or service significantly. People who don't want to think don't survive very long in this environment, but people with ideas and initiative thrive. Of course, you can imagine a scenario in which the boss abdicates his role entirely; that company will probably make little significant progress. The point is that it is possible to lead without suffocating talent, to entrust reliable helpers with significant responsibility, to rely on their capability and yet still answer for it. In general, overmanagement inhibits productivity; decentralized management enhances it.

Given the Bible's assertion that the Holy Spirit gifts every believer to serve the common good, which leadership style better allows this divine ministry to occur? Obviously, the second one does—the one that allows freer exercise of initiative and responsibility.

To treat members' gifts with integrity means that a church's leadership must trust that God intends to effect His purpose through those gifts. It means trusting the members. I try to help elders to realize that it's okay, for example, to express confidence in a certain ministry of the church even if you don't know exactly what shape that ministry is taking. Suppose a member comes to you, an elder, and says, "Did you know that the youth leader is taking the junior high kids on a retreat?" Not to know this does not represent failure on the elder's part or a breakdown of accountability. A proper response would be, "I didn't know that particular detail, but I know and support the youth leader's vision and ministry, and I have every confidence in his choices." An elder can have this kind of confidence when he knows that the ministry is being properly overseen.

But now, we do not rely on corporate America to provide our model of effective leadership. It merely corroborates the original model, God's own blueprint for leadership. The biblical picture of the elder dovetails perfectly with His double directive for the church. Let's take a look at this picture.

Questions for Discussion

1. Describe your church's leadership in light of the concepts discussed in this chapter:
   a. Do your leaders do everything?
   b. Do your leaders tell everybody what to do?
   c. Do you have no leadership?
   d. Do your leaders nurture the members' use of their gifts?
2. How many of your church members are aware of their own spiritual gifts? How many of them are using those gifts for the common benefit of the church?
3. In your church, how are the two important biblical directives balanced? What areas need to be addressed in order to enhance this balance?

Chapter 6 The Making of a Shepherd

Healthy Practice #3: The church must continuously train and implement shepherd leadership.

I reiterate emphatically: biblical church health virtually stands or falls with the health of the elders' ministry! You might think this strange; you might think that factors relating to elders would affect only elders, certainly not the remainder of the congregation (which is, of course, the larger portion of the church body). But now suppose you had a jigsaw puzzle with only two pieces. Looking at one piece, would you be able to tell the shape of the other? You would know it exactly. The point is that to specify the shape of the elders' ministry is to specify in a significant way the shape of the congregation's ministry.

For example, if the congregation perceives the elders as dictators, it will perceive itself as those who are dictated to. If it perceives the leadership as nonexistent, it will perceive itself as on its own, probably bereft of focus and unity. If it perceives the elders as shepherds along the lines of the biblical model, members will see themselves as sheep (in the best sense!): cared for, nurtured, following not by coercion but by desire, free to serve creatively in an orderly context.

You can guess that a congregation's perception at this

point drastically impacts its choices, its effectiveness, and its level of satisfaction. In my estimation, it affects how much God is able to use and bless that church.

My foremost wish for this chapter (and perhaps for this entire book!) is to communicate to you what it means for an elder to be a shepherd. The Bible explicitly offers this model as the norm. Jesus, God's ultimate leader and Head of the church, called Himself the Good Shepherd; God calls a church's leaders to be shepherds of His flock. Certainly He means for us to take this model seriously. I have seen over and over again how church health correlates with shepherd leadership. As elders strive to develop a shepherding relationship with members, that church's infrastructure develops into one that both allows divine directives (use of members' gifts, elders' orderly accounting) to be implemented, and allows God to work through it.

I realize that my readers bring to this discussion different levels of experience in church ministry. In order to put what I have to say on an even footing for all of you, I preface the heart of my message with a look at preliminary qualifications for the role of elder, the qualities of leadership, and what I call the mantle of accountability. The actual responsibilities belonging to the elder flow from the biblical concept of the elder as a shepherd, and these we'll consider in the next chapter.

I must make one preliminary comment with regard to the senior pastor. The reader who has examined the table of contents for this book may well have wondered about my emphasis on elders: I have no chapter on the pastor and more than one on elders! If you come from a denomination or a local church in which a solo pastor represents the totality of your church's leadership, where other leaders do little more than second the pastor's decisions and leave him to do the work (or are excluded from it), then for you the first step in grasping the Bible's conception of church health will be to realize that God intends us to ordain and count among His leaders both pastor and elders. Paul exhorts Timothy: "The elders who direct the affairs of the church well are worthy of double honor, especially those whose work is preaching and teaching" (1 Tim. 5:17). His words indicate that God intends there to be a plurality of elders, those officially entrusted with the spiritual oversight of the church, among whom are numbered elders whose work is preaching and teaching.

Thus, on the one hand, we need to avoid the error of conceiving of elders as insignificant; on the other hand, we need to avoid the error of conceiving of the pastor as distinct from, and superior to, the elders. I write to encourage elders, to heighten their sense of God's calling to their ministry, to help them to conceive of it along biblically healthy lines. But everything I say about elders in these chapters applies without distinction to the pastor, who is an elder among elders. There are some things to be said to pastors in later sections—pastors should not be indistinguishable from other elders—but these things only further specify the essentially *pastoral* ministry he shares with the elders.

Thus, just as everything in this book concerns the elders, so everything in this book concerns the pastor. It is profoundly significant that the pastor does not minister alone: he shepherds as part of a team, and he shepherds among a Spirit-gifted flock. As we look at the dynamics implied in these relationships, we see what God intends for the pastor.

Making the First Cut: Biblical Qualifications for Elders

How do you and your church know if God has called you to minister as an elder? Scripture describes the kind of person that God is looking for:

Now the overseer must be above reproach, the husband of but one wife, temperate, self-controlled, respectable, hospitable, able to teach, not given to drunkenness, not violent but gentle, not quarrelsome, not a lover of money. He must manage his own family well and see that his children obey him with proper respect. (If anyone does not know how to manage his own family, how can he take care of God's church?) He must not be a recent convert, or he may become conceited and fall under the same judgment as the devil. He must also have a good reputation with outsiders, so that he will not fall into disgrace and into the devil's trap. (1 Tim. 3: 2–7; see also Titus 1:5–9)

Some items in this list indicate positive gifts, skills, and attitudes that are essential to shepherding, such as the ability to teach and the ability to lead one's family with gentleness to orderly, respectful obedience. These conform to the shepherd model we'll discuss momentarily. However, most of the items listed here are stated negatively ("not quarrelsome," "not a recent convert"—hence, "elder," by the way!), leading us to think of this list as criteria for making "the first cut." If you demonstrate these qualities, your church can consider whether you might serve as an elder; if you don't demonstrate these qualities, then you cannot be considered for this ministry.

In this fallen world, not every man who now serves as an elder meets these qualifications. Over the years, I have seen biblically qualified elders, I have seen men in office who fail to meet these qualifications and recognize this fact, I have seen men in office who fail to recognize their lack of qualification, and I have seen men in office who don't qualify, who don't recognize it, who don't know what it means, and who don't care!

Of course, no one but Christ meets these qualifications perfectly. It helps to remember that they describe general patterns of behavior, not requirements of perfection.

It's important for every session of elders to plan for ongoing personal and group spiritual discipline, because all of us apart from the continual work of the Spirit through His Word and His church succumb to spiritual decay. And should your session include some of the less desirable sorts, regular spiritual maintenance is a good place to start.

It is also important to develop procedures to insure that those who are chosen to be elders do meet the biblical qualifications. I recommend the following plan to this end, which I have practiced in my own pastoral ministries and which I recommend as a consultant:

- Have members nominate men to be elders.
- For a period of several months, train these candidates, give them field experience, and pray together as a church for God's leading in the upcoming election.
- Conclude the training period with a gracious but careful evaluation by the session (which is the complete group of elders currently installed to serve) of each candidate's qualifications and maturity. Offer for the congregation's approval only those candidates whom the session evaluates positively.
- The congregation, with no power to make additional nominations, elects elders from among these trained and qualified candidates.
- This system effectively provides leadership that conforms to God's own qualifications.

Building Leadership Skills

The elder needs to meet biblical qualifications; he also needs to exhibit leadership skills, for shepherding is leading of a special kind. The Bible calls elders to be leaders: "Remember your leaders, who spoke the Word of God to you," says the writer to the Hebrews (13:7), as well as, "Obey your leaders and submit to their authority" (v. 17). In speaking to his young pastor friend, Timothy, Paul refers to the elders "who direct the affairs of the church" (1 Tim. 5:17).

"Joe's a born leader," we say, and we sometimes conclude tacitly that a person can't be a leader if he or she isn't born a leader. In reality, just about everybody leads with regard to some situation. And leadership, like any skill, can be learned and improved with analysis and practice.

Although the office of elder is restricted to men, leadership, even in the church, is not. It's important for the church to utilize the spiritual gifts of all its members, male and female. It's important that all members, male and female, sense the significance of their contribution. How this can work will become clear in chapter 8.

I offer the following facets of leadership on the basis of my study of Scripture, my experience, fieldwork, and reading. You won't find this list *per se* in Scripture, but you will find these characteristics displayed by the Bible's leaders and by Jesus *par excellence.*

Being a good leader involves developing what I call *personal disciplines:*

- You need to learn to *analyze* situations, goals, resources, and strategies *objectively.* This means that you try to elicit and consider all aspects, and to do so from other points of view besides your own.

- You need to *develop a system of feedback* concerning every situation—some legitimate avenue for confirming or disconfirming your perception. This both requires and furnishes wisdom; it also requires and heightens your credibility as a leader.
- You need to *invest yourself in other people,* especially in those who are potential leaders.
- You need to be willing to *put your insights into practice.* Simply being insightful does not amount to leadership. Insights need to be implemented in order to be effective.
- You need to possess and implicitly communicate *confidence.*
- You need to be confident of your own *personal focus,* the specific task and strategy to which God has called you at the present time.
- You need to be confident of your *desire* to serve in this capacity. For the elder, this means being sure that you desire to be an elder—a sign of God's calling you to this office (1 Tim. 3:1).
- You need to be confident that as you work, *the Holy Spirit plays the supreme role,* effecting all outcomes. You act and lead with confident expectation of supernatural involvement. This ought to be recognized in every human organization, since God is Lord of all. In the church, this reflects the all-important distinction between the organism and the organization, between the life and the ministry of the church: the latter of each pair represents the tangible structure that we shape and interact with; the former represents the intangible, but essential spiritual entity which *is* the church.

The Making of a Shepherd

- You need to be confident that you are *qualified,* that God has used and will use your leadership and your gifts. For the pastor, this includes confidence in the spiritual effectiveness of your preaching and teaching. This confidence is corroborated by the affirmation of the church.

The church sorely needs leaders who are confident that they are duly qualified. This confidence is not arrogance, although we can all think of examples of arrogant, immature leadership. But God Himself assures His chosen leaders that He will use them to get the work of His kingdom accomplished. All the spiritual gifts are given for the sake of the church, yet each is accompanied, in maturity, by the confidence that God is using that person's ministry in a supernatural way to accomplish His purposes.

Being a good leader involves naturally projecting certain *qualities of life:*

- You project *inspiration* for your vision—that is, for your idea about what is good for the group to do and be. People say, "He knows what he is talking about. The vision makes sense."
- You project *excitement* for your vision. People say, "I want to be part of this vision!"
- You project *confidence* in your leadership. People say, "I can trust this person's leadership."
- You project *sensitivity* to your followers. People say, "This person understands me and wants to hear from me."

A leader is *a mover and a shaker.* I've taken this idiom and utilized it to describe the ways a qualified leader goes about leading:

- You must be a *shaker,* a person who causes people to question the status quo. To get anything done, you have to incite people to be unhappy with their current circumstances, to see that the status quo is not enough. You also have to remove any barriers that prevent people from making changes. I do not mean to condone dissension or discontentment! But you will agree, I think, that as long as we remain sinful people, we can expect that the Holy Spirit will need to change us. The status quo will always be in need of improvement, both in our personal lives and in the life of the church body. Leadership, therefore, has to begin with Spirit-directed "shaking." Only then is there any need to go anywhere, any need for a leader to lead. And only then can there be spiritual growth.
- You must be a *mover* in the sense that you can influence people to strive toward a goal. Once people recognize the need to change, a leader uses his skills to encourage and enable them to move toward the goal.

A good leader must employ the following *skills:*

- You can *motivate* people. For people to be motivated to do anything, three things are needed. First, they must sense that their basic needs have been met, and that they are deemed significant people—that they are needed. Within the church, as we saw in chapter 4, the single greatest source of motivation is vital worship of the living God. This includes an ongoing sense of His presence and power, and it includes compelling preaching of His Word. Second, there must be a motivator, someone to get them moving. Third, there must be a plan for accomplishing the change. This will be our topic in part 3.

- You can *communicate* successfully. The process is complete only when the message has been understood.
- You can function as *an agent of change.* The agent of change is the one who gets and keeps people moving toward the common goal. Obviously this involves motivating people. Obviously it involves having a plan. But more is needed besides motivated people and a careful plan. I have in mind two things in particular: you must be able to resolve conflicts between people, and you must be able to delegate responsibility.

These leadership disciplines, qualities, and skills characterize anyone who leads, Christian or not. The Christian leader must recognize them and enhance them, relying on the Holy Spirit. The leader cannot take them for granted, but must project them if he or she is to be followed.

It doesn't take leadership training for you already to be practicing leadership. Stop and think of the times in your life when you "get people to do things," whether it's involving your children in yard work, campaigning for an election, or coaching a team.

The good news is that good leadership skills can in large measure be learned through ongoing training and assessment. A wise session plans for continuing education and mutual encouragement in this area. Leaders can and must constantly hone their skills in order to grow into God's plan for their leadership.

What Makes an Elder an Elder: Accountability

An elder is a leader of a special kind. A man who desires to be an elder or whose church desires him to be an elder presumably already demonstrates biblical qualifications and employs leadership skills. The difference between a biblically qualified leader and an elder is that God holds the elder officially accountable for the spiritual health of the church's members.

The book of Hebrews tells believers to obey their leaders and submit to their authority, for "they keep watch over you as men who must give an account" (13:17). God's message to the prophet Ezekiel demonstrates dramatically what it means to be accountable. God calls Ezekiel to be a watchman. He wants Ezekiel to warn His people about the mortal consequences of their sins. If Ezekiel warns the people and they do not heed the warning, they will die for their sins. And if Ezekiel fails to communicate God's warning, the people will still die, but God will also hold him accountable for their blood (Ezek. 3:16–21).

I often refer to accountability as a mantle or cloak. When God took the prophet Elijah to heaven, his cloak fell from him. His watching disciple, Elisha, picked up the cloak, an outward and graphic sign that he was assuming Elijah's ministry and claiming God's power and authority in the process (2 Kings 2). I see accountability as a mantle like Elisha's because God places it on the elder as he is ordained and because it has an outward dimension as well as an inward one.

Inwardly, God's Spirit works in the heart of the prospective elder, so that he longs to serve God's church in this capacity. Eldership is something that a man "sets his heart on," Paul says, and in doing so, he "desires a noble task" (1 Tim. 3:1). Inwardly, as we shall see, God shapes the elder into a shepherd.

Accountability in action is shepherding. Accountability is standing between God and the believer in order to lead the believer to know God's will more fully, to shape the believer's way of life (by the Holy Spirit's gracious work in the heart) to conform to this will, and to enable the believer to enjoy it.

The elder encourages believing church members to be what God intends them to be: priests (1 Peter 2:5), who utilize their gifts for the common good (1 Cor. 12:7), so that Christ's body is "joined and held together by every supporting ligament" (Eph. 4:16)—a people who "always carry around in our body the death of Jesus, so that the life of Jesus may also be revealed in our body" (2 Cor. 4:10). Paul expresses the elder's God-given passion to catalyze the church's growth in godliness: "We proclaim him, admonishing and teaching everyone with all wisdom, so that we may present everyone perfect in Christ. To this end I labor, struggling with all his energy, which so powerfully works in me" (Col. 1:28–29).

But accountability has a crucial outward aspect, also. The office of elder is a position conferred by God formally on a man through ordination. In this respect, eldership resembles citizenship, marriage, parenting, and political office. A wedding consists of a celebration of love; in this respect, nothing changes (hopefully!) after the wedding. But the wedding ceremony formalizes the relationship. After the marriage, certain legal and spiritual rights and privileges pertain which did not beforehand, no matter how much the couple was in love. Likewise, the office of parent entitles one to sign many forms as the person formally responsible for a child. It is possible for a formal marriage to exist in the absence of love. It is possible for another adult to act like a father or mother for a child when the child's real parents fail him or her in some way. Similarly, a brother or sister in Christ may offer effective spiritual encouragement. But the importance of these divinely granted inward realities does not imply that the official status is either useless or insignificant.

The office of elder indicates that oversight is God's own officially designated means for accomplishing the spiritual care of His children. This can be said equally of marriage and parenting. This is what it means to be ordained: God ordains or officially designates that man to serve as an elder. Others can shepherd, parent, or provide. Officially designated elders, spouses, or parents may fail. Nevertheless, it remains the case that the person occupying the office has a solemn, formal relationship to others before God. For elders, that relationship is accountability.

To say that God ordains a man to be an elder in no way denies that congregations determine that that man should serve. Again, we can understand how this works if we look at the institution of marriage. We choose partners for life on the basis of a careful assessment of various factors—from the passionately subjective to the coldly objective. The love stories of Scripture, such as Jacob and Rachel, and Ruth and Boaz, indicate that God expects and utilizes this procedure. The Bible also tells us that God ordains the institution. Husband and wife stand in a divinely designated relationship, to which God Himself attaches privileges and obligations. Human agency does not nullify God's ordination; rather, human agency serves as His instrument.

Here is the critical payoff: in his capacity as an elder, precisely because of God's official designation, the elder can expect His very real empowering for the task, just as Elisha, in taking the cloak, summoned the power of the God of Elijah.

As we look more closely at shepherding and all that it entails, we will in effect be exploring accountability. As we continue to elucidate a leadership strategy that blends elders' accountable oversight with members' gifted initiative, we will be exploring accountability. In turn, these discussions will specify what it means for the congregation to submit to this official leadership. When we explored the role of Word and worship in church life, we were exploring critical dimensions of the elders' accountability. In effect, this entire book fleshes out what it means for elders to be accountable in a biblically healthy way.

The Heart of It All: Elders Must Think like Shepherds

I'll never forget the moment, early in my ministry, when God first broke through my preconceived, totally inadequate notions to give me a glimpse of eldership as He meant it to be. He used a session of elders who knew what it meant to shepherd. One of those men was named Ted.

When I first came to the church, I saw myself as the pastor, and I viewed Ted as a banker who was an elder. I saw both of us performing church tasks and between us getting the job done. I thought our role as shepherds coincided with formal visits in the homes of members.

Just such an occasion occurred when one of our other elders died unexpectedly. Ted and I visited his widow on the night of his death. Friends and family had already begun to arrive. Food had materialized out of nowhere. The teenage sponsors were talking with the teenage boys. I wanted to say the right things in the midst of all this. I did use the right words and phrases. I believed that God was honored by my performance.

But Ted simply reached out and touched the widow's shoulder and said to her, "Jesus cares." I saw that with his simple statement and gesture, God was accomplishing much more than He had with my words. I recognized that this was because Ted was speaking out of an ongoing relationship with that church member. I saw that that relationship wasn't simply friendship or formal association with her husband. She was looking to him as one whose spiritual role it was to care for her soul, a status already in place through years of his ministry. I saw that this wasn't because Ted said the right words; it was because Ted cared about her personally and spiritually. He had actively integrated what for me was simply doctrine as he consciously lived out his role. He had demonstrated it for so long that it seemed to flow from the very core of his being. So when he spoke to this woman who was in shock, engulfed in anguish, God used his simple response to open the floodgates of her heart to begin His ministry of comfort and healing.

God was showing me that the essence of being an elder was this mind-set issuing in an official caring relationship. The Bible supplies the name: shepherding. Whatever else an elder says or does, whatever jobs he carries out, whatever words he utters, programs he administers, visits he pays, or decisions he makes, the orientation of his life and the heart of his ministry before God consist in shepherding the people whom God has entrusted to his care.

The essence of shepherding does not coincide exactly with anything programmable. It is not identical with the elder's various jobs and responsibilities, even those enjoined by Scripture. You can't capture it even by the sincere application of biblical doctrines to particular situations. It isn't guaranteed by election to the office. I don't mean to discount any of those things, but the essence of shepherding is intangible.

Although we cannot program it, we can reliably achieve it. An elder can achieve it by consciously living the shepherd role to which he has been ordained. He must concentrate his effort on learning and implementing shepherd care in everything he does. It takes constant prayer, availing oneself of the divine resources that accompany ordination. It takes constant meditation on Jesus' own model of shepherding. It takes the mutual encouragement and admonition of fellow elders. It takes the retooling of one's own thinking: "I am these people's shepherd; what does that require of me in this circumstance?"

The congregation's response to such shepherding is equally intangible. It is not identical to their formal submission to the elder's authority or their explicit obedience to the elder's direction. It is not reckoned in terms of the number of house calls a family has received. It is the comfort and assurance that they are shepherded, the emotional and spiritual security that frees a church member for eager spiritual growth and creative, happy service. It is natural and willing submission rather than artificial and grudging compliance.

Let me be clear: I believe that an elder who lives and thinks like a shepherd *will* project this to his flock; they will experience comfort and assurance as a result. Shepherding will be projected and assurance experienced, because of the elder's outlook, regardless of how many house calls he makes. Indeed, *only* when the elders embody this mind-set will a congregation sense shepherd leadership. Nothing else will substitute.

I have contemplated that moment with Ted for many years. I came to see that what I had perceived replicated God's model for church leadership. I became convinced that when sacrificial love and care motivate elders to enable the saints to grow in Christ, not only do those elders become in fuller measure the leaders God meant them to be, but also the congregation grows and serves in the way God meant them to. Members sense that their elders have devoted themselves to their spiritual welfare; they will respect this leadership and follow it freely and joyfully.

Because of its intangible nature, the essence of shepherding is hard to put into words, and it's best learned as it is modeled. Yet it is teachable and learnable. As you can see, I think that actualizing shepherd thinking is absolutely critical to the health of local churches. My personal passion is to help elders see this, to give them hope that they can achieve it, and to show them how it can be accomplished.

The Sad Facts About Shepherding

I have found that many churches make a mistake similar to mine when they identify shepherding with an elder visitation program. If elders plan regular (perhaps annual) visits with members, they presume that they can thereby accomplish the shepherding aspect of their job as elders.

But to think of shepherding as a programmable aspect of the elder's function is to misunderstand the elder's function completely. The elder is first of all a shepherd. Everything else that he does as an elder flows from this basic orientation. Biblical shepherding entails so much more than organized visitation; it is living a life that flows from a shepherd's heart.

What's more, a shepherding program becomes unworkable as a church membership grows. Even if, for the sake of argument, in a small church of twenty families, five elders could sustain a visitation program that allowed them significant involvement for spiritual influence, such involvement could be maintained as the church grew only if the number of elders increased accordingly. One hundred families would require twenty-five elders; two hundred families, fifty elders—an unrealistic number. We simply can't identify shepherding with visitation.

Sadly, the whole-souled shepherding that I first glimpsed in Ted and his colleagues is the exception rather than the norm. In my ministry as a consultant, one of the questions I ask members and elders is this: "Are the elders shepherding the members to grow in faith?" (I do not ask, "How many official calls at church members' homes have you logged?") After many years of studying churches, my basic conclusion is that church members seldom believe they are being shepherded. I have also concluded that some elders sincerely believe they are shepherding the church, even though the members do not perceive it. The third, and perhaps most revealing, conclusion is that most elders admit that they are failing to shepherd. Consequently, shepherding is most often the missing component that elders need to enable them to lead the church body into a high degree of spiritual maturity and health.

God's Shepherd

There is always good news! Once you have identified a missing component, you have taken the first step toward rectifying the situation. What's more, God Himself has supplied the blueprint and the "floor model" to train those whom He has called to lead. As we look at this blueprint in the Word, and as we examine the Lord's personal example, the Holy Spirit can effect in and through us the vital ministry of shepherding.

The Lord teaches the children of Israel to think of Him as a shepherd. "The LORD is my shepherd," David writes in the best loved of Psalms. Jacob speaks of Him as "the God who has been my shepherd all my life to this day" (Gen. 48:15; cf. 49:24; Pss. 28:9; 80:1; Eccl. 12:11; Isa. 40:11; Jer. 31:10; Ezek. 34:12, 16). Throughout His revelation in the Old Testament, God also uses the shepherd as a model for human leadership.

His directive to Israel's shepherd-turned-king, David is: "You will shepherd my people Israel" (2 Sam. 5:2; cf. 7:7; 1 Chron. 11:2; 17:6; Ps. 78:71; Isa. 63:11). His description of the people's direst plight is that they are "like sheep without a shepherd" (Num. 27:17; cf. 1 Kings 22:17; 2 Chron. 18:16; Isa. 13:14; 63:11; Ezek. 34:5, 8; Zech. 10:2; 11:17; 13:7; Mark 6:34). Jesus, God's Messiah, the pinnacle of God's self-revelation, is the Shepherd of shepherds—in prophecy, in self-reference, and in New Testament descriptions (Ezek. 37:24; Mic. 5:4; Matt. 2:6; 26:31; Mark 14:27; John 10:1–18; Heb. 13:20; 1 Peter 2:25; 5:4; Rev. 7:17). And here's an awesome irony in the metaphor: the Great Shepherd of the sheep is none other than the Lamb!

And now God has called elders to a shepherding ministry: "To the elders among you . . . : Be shepherds of God's flock that is under your care . . . [until] the Chief Shepherd appears" (1 Peter 5:1–4). The *elders* are to be *shepherds* of *God's flock* until *the Chief Shepherd* appears! What an awesome privilege it is to join Israel's kings, Jesus the Savior, and the Father Himself in the metaphor! It is evident that He means to shepherd His own flock, the church, officially through His undershepherds, the elders of the church.

As individual "sheep," we have listened to and loved Christ's words about shepherding in John 10. "I am the Good Shepherd," He says, ministering spiritual comfort and assurance to each of us. But when it becomes apparent that elders are first and foremost shepherds carrying out God's shepherding, Christ's words compel a fresh look. We return to follow the Chief Shepherd, not only as sheep, but also as apprentice shepherds. "Treat them the way I treat them, the way I have treated you. You want to lead? Make Me your model. The sheep need to perceive you the way they perceive Me."

The Making of a Shepherd   137

In light of this literally "pastoral" calling, consider the Chief Shepherd's address (John 10:1–18):

> "I tell you the truth, the man who does not enter the sheep pen by the gate, but climbs in by some other way, is a thief and a robber. The man who enters by the gate is the shepherd of his sheep. The watchman opens the gate for him, and the sheep listen to his voice. He calls his own sheep by name and leads them out. When he has brought out all his own, he goes on ahead of them, and his sheep follow him because they know his voice. But they will never follow a stranger; in fact, they will run away from him because they do not recognize a stranger's voice." Jesus used this figure of speech, but they did not understand what he was telling them.

> Therefore Jesus said again, "I tell you the truth, I am the gate for the sheep. All who ever came before me were thieves and robbers, but the sheep did not listen to them. I am the gate; whoever enters through me will be saved. He will come in and go out, and find pasture. The thief comes only to steal and kill and destroy; I have come that they may have life, and have it to the full.

> "I am the good shepherd. The good shepherd lays down his life for the sheep. The hired hand is not the shepherd who owns the sheep. So when he sees the wolf coming, he abandons the sheep and runs away. Then the wolf attacks the flock and scatters it. The man runs away because he is a hired hand and cares nothing for the sheep.

> "I am the good shepherd; I know my sheep and my sheep know me—just as the Father knows me and I

know the Father—and I lay down my life for the sheep. I have other sheep that are not of this sheep pen. I must bring them also. They too will listen to my voice, and there shall be one flock and one shepherd. The reason my Father loves me is that I lay down my life—only to take it up again. No one takes it from me, but I lay it down of my own accord. I have authority to lay it down and authority to take it up again. This command I received from my Father."

Caring, loving, equipping—these three words express the essence of Christ's lesson about shepherding. A good shepherd is one whose care for the sheep drives him to equip them for doing what sheep do best, even at the cost of his own life.

The Shepherd/Elder Cares for His Charges

The shepherd cares for his sheep. I first visualize the shepherd carrying a sheep. Some popular paintings capture this view and feed our visual image. But God fosters it Himself, for Isaiah 40:11 describes the Lord like this:

> He tends his flock like a shepherd:
>> He gathers the lambs in his arms
> and carries them close to his heart;
>> he gently leads those that have young.

This picture expresses both the strength and the tenderness of a person who very much cares for someone and is in a position to help. The same quality meets us in Jesus' description of the Good Shepherd. Here is a leader who loves, not one who is merely discharging obligations. The picture expresses the precious intangible reality we're after when we talk of shepherding. As you meditate on the following aspects of shepherding, keep the image of *carrying* in your mind.

He bears God's official accreditation. The shepherd/elder "enters by the gate," unlike "thieves and robbers." God has accredited him to shepherd His flock. This hints at an official mantle of accountability.

He initiates the relationship. The shepherd/elder "calls his own sheep by name." As God the Father unilaterally initiated a relationship with us before the foundation of time (what grace!), so the undershepherd initiates a shepherding relationship with individual members.

He plans and protects. The shepherd/elder "leads them out," presumably to protected pasture and water. Food and water for sheep, Word and Spirit for believers—the elders see to it that these are amply provided. For the elder/shepherds, this translates into good planning. To guarantee an ample supply of spiritual food, water, and protection, the session must make plans to provide them. I often find that elders are failing to plan for either the short term or the long term. As a result, members exhibit the kind of insecurity that one attributes to weak leadership. I encourage sessions to make a practice of planning practical strategies for meeting goals. I encourage them to do this, not at regular meetings, but at special meetings. We'll talk about this more later.

God expects elders to protect believers from wolves, from Satan—from temptation and heresy. As we'll see, one of the elders' critical responsibilities is to guard the members. Paul tells the young elder Timothy to "guard what has been entrusted to your care" (1 Tim. 6:20; cf. 2 Tim. 1:14), indicating both the retention of sound doctrine and the ongoing assessment of the spiritual welfare of his charges. Guarding involves monitoring the teaching and preaching of the Word to guarantee its faithfulness to Scripture. It also involves seeing to it that believers keep away from temptation and continue walking close to God. Sometimes it involves church discipline.

This is spiritual care at work, a ministry so complete that the sheep know that they will "come in and go out, and find pasture." Members can confidently and joyfully expect that their spiritual needs will be met with pure doctrine and vital ministry as the elders guard these central aspects of church life.

He gives life itself. The elder/shepherd does not furnish only the daily needs of food, water, and protection. He also furnishes life itself: "I am the gate; whoever enters through me will be saved. . . . I have come that they may have life, and have it to the full." Christ alone calls forth life from death, for He alone has the power of life in Himself. But the elder/shepherd points the sinner to Christ, offering unqualified assurance of abundant life, not on any merit of his own, but entirely because of the reliable, gracious Word of God.

He leads in outreach. "I have other sheep that are not of this sheep pen. I must bring them also. They too will listen to my voice, and there shall be one flock and one shepherd." This verse makes me shout for joy, for I was one of those "other sheep"! How glad each of us is that the Great Shepherd did not rest content with His flock, but actively added to it! Shepherd/elders' care extends to people not yet a part of the flock. This speaks to any temptation we might feel to keep the care-giving relationship for ourselves and not share it with others. Sometimes in our insecurity we fear that adding others to the care group will reduce the benefits that we receive. But any healthy group knows that love deepens as it multiplies. Elders must follow the Lord's example of reaching out to bring others into the fold.

A church I pastored invited a local director of a Messianic Center to speak. I was touched and challenged by what he said: he exhorted us never to feel that the gospel cannot reach different segments of people because of who they are or what they're like. If everybody had thought that way, he said simply, "No one would have found me." The Lord does work with people we'd never expect to embrace the gospel.

Elder/shepherds encourage and equip those under their care to reach out to the lost, and to do so in confident expectation that God is at work to complete His church. Also, they lead the flock to assimilate newcomers. This means that new believers become integrally situated in the mesh of body life, both receiving and initiating spiritual ministry: the Lord envisions *one* flock.

Undershepherds can show members that outreach is a natural extension of following the Good Shepherd's model. Jesus sees the eternal picture. He has chosen other sheep. He gave His life to secure their future, just as He gave His life for ours. He calls us to share His perspective and mission. He promises a harvest as we serve faithfully. Zechariah prophesies: "This is what the LORD Almighty says: 'In those days ten men from all languages and nations will take firm hold of one Jew by the hem of his robe and say, "Let us go with you, because we have heard that God is with you"'" (Zech. 8:23). Would you huddle in the shelter when in Christ the world lies at your feet?

He inspires happy submission. Here's the part that clues us in concretely about leadership style. The elder/shepherd's legitimacy and acceptance as a leader grow out of this caring relationship. The sheep follow the shepherd "because they know his voice." In their woolly minds, the shepherd's call signals carefree feasting, peaceful slumber, and TLC. He does not drive them ahead; they follow willingly behind. They are not being coerced, but are freely choosing a reliable delight. In the church, members should follow the lead of elders, not because the elders tell them what to do, but because the elders have cared for them. What the members should feel is not compulsion, but care.

He fosters implicit trust. "I know my sheep and my sheep know me." The essence of successful elder shepherding is heart-to-heart bonding that leads to complete, mutual confidence, born of intimate knowledge. This personal dimension of the undershepherd's ministry causes the congregation's implicit trust in him as their shepherd to grow, as they experience the depth of his commitment to them. Members don't simply know him as a leader; they know him and trust him completely. The elder does not think of the members simply as recipients of spiritual nourishment; he knows them, and he relies on them as God uses them in his and the church's life. This results in a priceless, joyful way of life for the whole group.

The Shepherd/Elder Loves Sacrificially

Just how much the shepherd/elder cares for his charges is demonstrated by the lengths to which he will go on their behalf. Sacrificial love is care raised to the nth power. "The good shepherd lays down his life for the sheep" (John 10:11). The elder cares so deeply for those for whom God holds him accountable that he never gives up on the sheep. He keeps on serving, even at great cost to himself. "Love never fails," Paul says (1 Cor. 13:8). Note that sacrificial love marks not only the best elder-member relationship, but also the best marriage and family relationships. In a real sense, we can expect the former to look like the latter. Note also that, for this quality to be recognized in the elder by the member, a deep, program-transcending interpersonal relationship must have been established. Usually those who can say with the shepherd, "I know him, and he knows me," are the people who have witnessed sacrificial love.

Often this sacrificial love must be sustained over years, and even then we should never give up. In my church, there was a family whose daughter attended a denominationally related college. Sadly, strife instigated by the college's leadership virtually destroyed that young woman's education. Her father, one of our deacons, became deeply bitter. I began to visit him and pray with him one to three times a week. I ended up doing that for years. God finally chose to break down his bitterness. When you don't give up, the Holy Spirit, on His timetable, does His thing. Your job is to keep at it: love *never* fails.

The Shepherd/Elder Equips Members for Growth and Ministry

All of this effort on the sheep's behalf adds up to a wonderful arrangement for the sheep! If we look at the caring activity of the shepherd/elder from the point of view of the sheep, we see that the shepherd/elder's ministry of care and love is one that equips and enables the sheep/members to flourish spiritually. They choose joyfully to follow a leader accredited by God's official ordination and by that shepherd's evident care for them. They rely confidently on the shepherd/elder's well-planned provision. They rest secure because he guards them from danger. They trust his leadership because they know him and know he knows them. They join him in reaching out to others.

It is important to see that all these wonderful benefits do not do for the sheep what the sheep are meant to do for themselves. Rather, they furnish an optimal environment in which the sheep can grow and flourish. If you want a luxuriant garden of flowers or vegetables, you must nurture it with well-tilled soil, proper acid levels, moisture, fertilizer, weed removal, etc. But these things don't cause the actual growing, which remains God's miracle. You can't force the rose or the rutabaga to grow. What you do is to give it the environment that you know is best in order for it to be its best. The same applies to flocks of sheep. Shepherds provide the safe environment. Secure sheep are sheep that produce wool, lambs, and meat. In other words, elders nurture church life, but cannot produce it. Their goal is the spiritual growth and ministry of their members, and this they can encourage and enhance, but cannot program. I like the word *equip*, for it indicates that the person being equipped is about to initiate a task which the equipper cannot do for himself. A healthy church keeps the mutuality of this relationship in view.

At the beginning of this discussion, I said that the shape of the elders' ministry affects the entire church body. What it means to be an elder depends on how he relates to members. As the elders endeavor to create an optimal environment for members' spiritual growth, they might over- or undershoot the balance indicated by the shepherd model. Suppose a church's elders do very little planning, or monitoring of doctrinal purity, or informal nurturing of the saints. That would leave the members like sheep without a shepherd. Yes, the sheep can exercise initiative, but in the absence of a shepherd's foresight, the results may be disastrous. Advance will be disorganized and slow at best.

Suppose the other extreme exists: shepherds mistakenly think they can or ought to do everything for the sheep. This sad scenario occurs when elders believe that they must make every decision affecting church life if they are to be properly accountable to God. Some churches give the impression that the session expects that it can program spirituality, and that spirituality, in fact, is to be identified with participation in all of the church's programs.

These two extremes correspond to what we saw in chapter 5 in connection with God's double directive for church leadership. The one extreme excludes the directive of elder accountability; the other excludes the directive concerning members' initiative in exercising the Spirit's gifts. As I said, God calls elders to lead and guide this Spirit-assembled mix of Spirit-bestowed gifts. Elders must remember that God Himself made the mix; elders should never attempt to replace the church's ministry with their own. The shepherd model for elders' ministry allows both directives to be maintained in a natural equilibrium. In my estimation, it promotes the fullest measure of church health, the Holy Spirit's work, and God's blessing. This state of affairs is Spirit driven—not people driven or staff driven, the two extremes that churches need to steer between.

I can remember when the light came on for one church to which I was presenting this concept of shepherding. It was when I met with the elders and deacons together, and stressed that the work of a deacon is fundamentally a ministry of mercy, and that the diaconate serves integrally in the organic life of the church. That church had suffered from a common misperception that deacons are bankers and lawn caretakers. They began to see that the deacons had a spiritual calling of a different sort. The deacons' fresh perception of themselves as doing something spiritually significant, making decisions and helping people, liberated them to minister. Deacons ought to be doing more than handling money; they have to deal with people and their problems.

In that church, the elders had been directing everything, and had restricted deacons to money management. Now the elders began to encourage the deacons to exercise their proper biblical office. This expanded that church's utilization of the Spirit's gifts to members. It precipitated an ongoing transformation of that church's spiritual vitality.

Admittedly, in many churches, the prospect of deacons actually doing something would scare the elders to death! Moving toward the biblical model takes prayer, courage, and trust—trust in God, and trust in His work in and through all members' gifts.

Not every church that attempts to make this change is successful. I can think of one church which, when I am present with them, seems ready and able to move in the right direction. But the elders aren't really ready to break the mold of what the church has done for many years. This kind of problem often occurs in a smaller session, where one person exercises control and resists such change. The rest aren't going to oppose him. In a larger session, with greater diversity, this kind of opposition to change occurs less frequently.

How to Actualize the Shepherd Outlook

What can you do if your ministry or that of other elders on your session fails to live up to this shepherd model? First, as I said before, take heart: you are already farther along than elders who do not even recognize their inadequacy! Recognizing the need is the first big step toward rectifying matters.

Building this mind-set requires the same activities as maintaining it. This means that all elders, at every stage of shepherd maturity, must be doing the same things. Simply stated, they are:

- Meditate, individually and as a session, on this model of Christ's. It is most helpful for each man to submit a paper in which he expresses how his personal calling by God to shepherd His people permeates and drives all of his life. As he lives as a Christian, trusting and obeying in all aspects of his life, he is modeling the Christian life for his people and encouraging them in their walk. This is the sort of thing that parents and teachers understand well—simultaneous living and guiding.
- Pray, individually and as a session, for the Holy Spirit to actualize the shepherd model in all aspects of your life and ministry.
- Develop a strategy to hold one another accountable to think and minister like shepherds.
- Devise and implement plans that actualize this kind of mind-set and ministry. For example, devote regular meetings to these activities; limit other formal involvement—both elders' and members'—so as to concentrate on the intangible reality of shepherd leadership.
- Devise a way to assess your efforts. How can you tell if you are succeeding at shepherding? You will have been successful shepherds if the "sheep" report that

they are being carried by the Good Shepherd Himself. They will report that *God* gathers them in His arms and carries them close to His heart (Isa. 40:11). They should grow in their awareness of God's love and faithfulness. They should be testifying with the words of the psalmist, "Great is your love, reaching to the heavens; your faithfulness reaches to the skies" (Ps. 57:10). Your session must devise a practical way to listen regularly to the sheep for this testimony.

I have counseled churches to kick off this effort through a weekend of in-depth Bible study and prayer. At this time, elders pair off to form accountability partnerships. Each man prays for the other. And as each strives to implement a shepherd outlook, taking the steps specified in the workshop, he can anticipate reporting to his partner in three months' time. Within a year, the entire group should meet together to share. This kind of mutual accountability can be ongoing.

I've had very favorable responses from churches that have taken this seriously. It is humbling and encouraging to think of the caliber of men who are doing this: a vice president of a hospital chain, a prominent architect, a university law professor, an electrical engineering consultant, and several ministers.

The making of a shepherd and the keeping of a shepherd require employing these disciplines, not for a finite period of training, but as a way of life. Wherever you and your session are on the "growth chart," and however the congregation currently perceives your ministry, put these disciplines into practice now.

Questions for Discussion

1. Gauge your own church's shepherding outlook:
    a. Do members perceive that they are being shepherded?
    b. Do elders believe that they are shepherding?
2. What evidence can you supply to support your assessments in question 1?
3. What factors currently prevent your church from developing a richer shepherding ministry?
4. What steps can you take to follow God's call to shepherd ministry?

Chapter 7 The Elder's Official Responsibilities

So far, we've talked about basic qualifications for being an elder and basic leadership skills. We've discussed what it means for elders to be accountable for church members. I trust that I've made my case that the shepherd model shapes the elder's ministry from the roots of his being to the things he says and does, and that the session should fashion an optimal environment for the congregation's spiritual growth and ministry.

Now Scripture explicitly directs elders to carry out certain activities. When I work with church sessions, I utilize the acrostic G-O-E-S to help elders identify and group their responsibilities as guardian, overseer, example, and shepherd.

Now that we have explored in depth the biblical model of the elder as shepherd, we see that these official activities are natural outward expressions of that inward orientation. We've already discussed these responsibilities in some measure as we explored the shepherd metaphor. But God does not leave us to figure them out solely on the basis of the metaphor. These four tasks come with His direct command, as we'll see. The correlation between the shepherd model that shapes the elder's inward approach and the specific commands that direct his outward activity demonstrates the profound integrity of Scripture, as well as confirming the rightness of this concept of the elder's ministry.

G—Guardian

> *Keep watch* over yourselves and all the flock of which the Holy Spirit has made you overseers. . . . I know that after I leave, savage wolves will come in among you and will not spare the flock. Even from your own number men will arise and distort the truth in order to draw away disciples after them. So be on your *guard!* (Acts 20:28–31)

> *Watch* your life and doctrine closely. Persevere in them, because if you do, you will save both yourself and your hearers. (1 Tim. 4:16)

> Timothy, *guard* what has been entrusted to your care. Turn away from godless chatter and the opposing ideas of what is falsely called knowledge, which some have professed and in so doing have wandered from the faith. (1 Tim. 6:20–21)

> What you heard from me, *keep* as the pattern of sound teaching, with faith and love in Christ Jesus. *Guard* the good deposit that was entrusted to you—*guard* it with the help of the Holy Spirit who lives in us. (2 Tim. 1:13–14)

The church of Jesus Christ is by definition a group of people who believe certain statements to be true. In a real sense, if you change the statements—if you add to them, subtract from them, deny some of them, or "tweak" them—you no longer have the church of Jesus Christ. The Bible insists on this tight definition of the church, because the words of God, in Scripture and in Christ, are all-important. They are life itself (John 1:1–5; Ps. 119:105, 116). The passages quoted above only state explicitly what Scripture enjoins or implies throughout.

Since a doctrinally impure church fails to be a fully viable church of Jesus Christ, and since it fails to match the life-giving Word of God, guarding against the encroachment of error constitutes a most critical responsibility. It is a mistake to assume that a church (like an individual) will remain in its original orthodox condition apart from ongoing Spirit-induced reform, for the undertow of sin continually drags us toward false belief and practice. God allots to elders the task of preserving the doctrinal integrity of the church and its members.

The New Testament church received regular apostolic warnings to guard against false doctrine creeping in through, generally, two ports of entry: teachers or preachers, and concrete application of the message. "Watch out for false prophets," Jesus warns (Matt. 7:15), and the apostles repeatedly cry out against this subtle source of spiritual death (2 Peter 2; Jude 4; Gal. 4:17). They also summon churches to spiritual and doctrinal maturity, so that they will remain invulnerable to "every wind of teaching" and "the cunning and craftiness of men in their deceitful scheming" (Eph. 4:14). To do this, they must "live a life worthy of the calling you have received," "put on the new self," and "be imitators of God" (4:1, 24; 5:1). And churches are helped in this by leaders who are gifted by the Spirit to be evangelists, pastors, and teachers (4:11).

Any church, in whatever century, must guard these two ports. The elders must be sure that the church is teaching the Bible as God's revelation of truth, and they must be sure that members continue to live in accordance with the Word.

The Elder's Official Responsibilities

Guarding the Word. In regard to preaching and teaching, the elders need to insure that members receive "the truth, the whole truth, and nothing but the truth." On the one hand, it is necessary to communicate the whole truth, which we sometimes call "the whole counsel of God" (Acts 20:27 KJV)—that is, everything that the Bible teaches. It's important that we teach from all the books of the Bible, as well as the whole system of doctrine contained in the Bible.

Pastors and church teachers can easily fall into one of three traps. First, they can fail to study the Word of God in depth. Laziness, busyness, and presumed familiarity with a passage can lead a preacher or teacher to prepare inadequately. The inevitable result is, at best, a shallow and lifeless presentation. At worst, it can be an imbalanced and even erroneous portrayal of God's mind. It takes time and study to grasp the Word in its profundity. Elders must insure, for example, that pastors and teachers take the time and do the studying necessary to communicate the whole truth of Scripture.

Second, pastors and teachers can fall into the trap of communicating only the message of salvation. This fails to provide members with the well-balanced spiritual diet necessary for them to mature. And maturity is definitely the goal in view: Paul says that God gifts pastors and teachers "to prepare God's people . . . until we all reach unity in the faith and in the knowledge of the Son of God and become mature, attaining to the whole measure of the fullness of Christ" (Eph. 4:12–13). Elders must see to it that pastors' sermon series address all aspects of biblical teaching and Christian living, and that Sunday school and small groups proceed in orderly fashion through the Scriptures.

Third, pastors and teachers can fall into the trap of riding a hobbyhorse. It's easy to fall in love with a single doctrine that has revolutionized our personal spirituality. Sometimes it takes the objectivity of others to help us avoid talking about it to the exclusion of other truths. Elders officially provide this objective outlook, thus guarding the teaching of God's Word.

In a church in western Pennsylvania some years ago, the pastor began to preach on the sovereignty of God. He expounded Scripture faithfully as he presented it. The people all came to agree with the message he preached and rejoiced to apply it in realistic ways in their lives. Unfortunately, he preached on the same subject every Sunday for a full year! Within the year, almost half of the congregation left to start a second church not far away. When asked the reason for their departure, they responded that they felt inadequately fed. During the following years, neither church grew well.

On the other hand, it is necessary to preach nothing but the truth. Thus, the elders must guard against heresy. Every believer, including a pastor or teacher, is still growing spiritually. This applies to his understanding, so that his comprehension of a verse or passage may not be entirely accurate. Also, a pastor, for all the sincerity of his commitment to Christ and Scripture, may come to espouse error unintentionally and gradually. Elders offer continual "product quality control."

Historically, the church has been tempted to accommodate its teaching to prevailing worldviews and cultural commitments. It can be extremely difficult to distinguish Scripture's teaching from our particular society's mind-set, immersed as we are in it. To guard against this calls for wisdom deeply rooted in the Word, as well as perception of cultural and historical trends. Theology is God's truth applied. Its application requires awareness of that to which it is applied.

All this obviously assumes that elders themselves know the

The Elder's Official Responsibilities

Bible and its doctrines well enough to spot not only falsehood, but also imbalance. You can see that preparing men to serve as elders must include in-depth study of Scripture and its doctrines. The goal is not achieved by providing prospective elders with a course of theological study, although such a course can be a wonderful tool. The goal, according to Scripture, is for an elder to be "able to teach" (1 Tim. 3:2). This man knows the Bible and its system of doctrine well enough to discern the real issues involved in members' problems, programs, and decisions, and he can apply the Bible accurately to them.

Also, this indicates the need for someone to hold elders themselves accountable in these matters. In my denomination, each elder vows agreement to a certain understanding of what the Bible teaches (the Westminster Confession of Faith). He also vows to examine his own views continually and to make known any personal deviations from "the fundamentals of this system." Plus, teaching elders (pastors), ruling elders, and the church they represent constitute a larger group, called the presbytery, to whom they are answerable. This larger structure acts as yet another safeguard to maintain the purity of the teaching of the church.

Guarding the sheep. Positively, the elders ensure that members are growing in Christ. This coincides with the shepherds' nurturing ministry, which offers every spiritual blessing to the sheep: teaching, discipling, worship, fellowship, the sacraments, diaconal care and comfort, and all the benefits of vital participation in the body of Christ.

Negatively, the elders discourage members from pursuing sinful practices. This coincides with church discipline. Unfortunately, we usually identify church discipline with its most extreme and public outcome, excommunication. In a real sense, however, church discipline is a ministry of nurturing that extends through all phases of guarding.[1] The first phase is the most critical and is usually all that is necessary. It consists of informal interpersonal relationships that encourage righteousness and discourage sin. A church's leaders can foster the development of these relationships. This addresses personal sin.

A church must also equip its members to deal with interpersonal sin, so as to prevent its spread. Jesus teaches us how to handle offenses. If I have offended someone, and I am sensitive enough to recognize this, I must initiate reconciliation (Matt. 5:23–24). If someone else has offended me, I must also initiate discussion to seek reconciliation (Matt. 18:15–18). If church members faithfully practiced these methods, so much heartbreaking and destructive dissension could be eliminated! Only after individuals have attempted these overtures without success should formal church discipline occur.

This means that one of the most important things that elders can do is to teach their charges to practice these informal procedures. They can also decline to act formally on any matter in which these prior steps have not been taken. They may even administer formal discipline to the individual who refuses to take them!

In any matter such as this, the elder/shepherd's manner must be gentle (Gal. 6:1), his goal must be restoration, and his motive may never be one of personal vindication (1 Cor. 10:31).

To summarize: God calls a church's elders to guard the Word and the members. The former involves preserving doctrinal purity and balance; the latter entails encouraging spiritual growth and discouraging sin.

The Elder's Official Responsibilities   157

O—Overseer

Here is a trustworthy saying: If anyone sets his heart on being an *overseer*, he desires a noble task. (1 Tim. 3:1)

An *overseer* is entrusted with God's work. (Titus 1:7)

Keep watch over yourselves and all the flock of which the Holy Spirit has made you *overseers*. (Acts 20:28)

Be shepherds of God's flock that is under your care, serving as *overseers*—not because you must, but because you are willing, as God wants you to be; . . . not lording it over those entrusted to you, but being examples to the flock. (1 Peter 5:2–3)

The elders who *direct* the affairs of the church well are worthy of double honor, especially those whose work is preaching and teaching. (1 Tim. 5:17)

Obey your *leaders* and submit to their authority. They keep watch over you as men who must give an account. Obey them so that their work will be a joy, not a burden, for that would be of no advantage to you. (Heb. 13:17)

Being an elder consists almost by definition of overseeing. The New Testament often calls the elder an overseer. What makes an elder an elder, as I said before, is the mantle of accountability, the fact that God has officially ordained him to answer for a group of believers' spiritual well-being. Oversight and accountability go hand in hand.

The writer of Hebrews beseeches his readers to follow their leaders willingly, making their job of giving an account to God easy and joyful. This request indicates that those who lead do so, not by executive order, but by exercising authority that is freely acknowledged, that grows out of the nurturing, sacrificial love that the elder demonstrates toward those in his care.

It's useful to distinguish between authority and power. Authority is the right to be obeyed. Power is the ability to effect another's compliance, even against his or her will. The Greek word for "power" in the New Testament is *dynamis,* which is used to refer to God's power as expressed in mighty works and miracles, including Jesus' resurrection and the Spirit's work in our lives. The Greek word *exousia* refers to authority, a right to be obeyed. God gives authority to elders to care for His people. He intends His people to follow their leadership willingly, not because they have been coerced. The only legitimate power in the church is the power of Christ, working in and through His people, members and officers together. It is not the power of the officers over the members. Power is God's work. Too often men mistakenly believe that they must coerce the congregation into compliance. When elders practice shepherdlike oversight and members practice willing submission, the Holy Spirit's power is unleashed to accomplish God's purposes.

Some elders confuse power with authority. Being determined not to exercise "raw power," they avoid authoritative leadership, or at least fail to lead with any confidence. Others, determined to account properly to God for their charges, muscle them into obedience. The confusion between authority and power parallels the failure to distinguish between accountability and responsibility, which we discussed in chapter 5.

Inextricably related to their task of exercising oversight is the elders' responsibility to plan for the spiritual welfare of the church. In Hebrews 13:7, 17, 24, "leaders" translates a form of the Greek word *hegomai*, which means "lead, guide, govern." Similarly, in 1 Timothy 5:17 Paul describes the elders as those who direct the affairs of the church. (Note, by the way, that this passage teaches that a plurality of elders govern together, and that the group includes, but is not limited to, those who preach and teach, and that some compensation is appropriate.) This calls for planning and administration, just as the shepherd looks ahead and leads his flock with a view to optimal food, water, and safety.

Sensible, sensitive planning. Much of what I have to say about planning relates to my strategy for articulating and implementing a church's specific vision, which I address in part 3. But a few things can be said at this point.

First, as we've already seen, whatever planning and administration may involve, they do not involve the elders doing all the work of ministry and making all the decisions, excluding any significant use of members' spiritual gifts. In the next chapter, I'll offer my concrete strategy for keeping the two divine directives balanced.

Second, a church session must engage in both short-term and long-term planning, but these should never be attempted at routine meetings. Devote routine meetings to prayer, shepherding, and making operational decisions. Call special meetings to focus exclusively on planning.

Third, people should never be asked to vote on plans immediately after they have been unveiled. Instead, publicize your proposals in time for members to pray about them and discuss them. Worthwhile proposals survive this process; weaknesses will become evident in time to revise them.

Fourth, work overtime on communication. As you publicize your plan, tell the details, possibly several times, possibly both orally and in writing. When you have done this, you're still only half-finished. You need to take steps to make sure that members understand what they've heard.

These last two strategies don't come from a specific Bible passage. They're the sort of thing that any good leader understands and implements. But please note that they typify a leadership style that demonstrates respect for the followers. Scripture certainly envisions this approach, rather than one that would demean the followers. Such an approach does justice to the Spirit's directives for both accountable leadership and the integrity of members' gifts.

Good, Spirit-conformed leadership strategies can be learned, and you can expect to rely on "continuing education" and mutual encouragement to keep leadership skills well honed.

Active administration. Administration involves organizing, scheduling, expediting, following through, and evaluating. I will be saying more about administration in later chapters, but let me speak here once again of the elders' role as the agents of change in the life of the church.

Whenever a process involves a plurality of persons, people in leadership must know how to be agents of change. Sometimes fear or complacency has stalled progress. Sometimes an obstacle, real or perceived, looms ahead. Sometimes it is simply the time to get moving on a new course. An agent of change can find a gracious and loving way to lead people to realize that the status quo is unsatisfactory. I've referred to this as "shaking."

The agent of change must also be prepared for "moving." The elder must have developed a strategy or proposal for remedying the situation. It must reflect adequate research of the problem, adequate awareness of the consequences of employing it, and a reasonable expectation of the time it will take to explain, sell, and implement it. When the agent of change offers his proposal, he should explain it thoroughly, answer objections, and encourage the necessary action.

Being able to effect change is a key tool in the leader's kit. Leaders rely on it often to keep people and affairs moving toward the desired goal. That's why it relates to administration.

E—Example

> Be shepherds of God's flock that is under your care, serving as overseers . . . not lording it over those entrusted to you, but being *examples* to the flock. (1 Peter 5:2–3)

> In everything set them an *example* by doing what is good. (Titus 2:7)

> Don't let anyone look down on you because you are young, but set an *example* for the believers in speech, in life, in love, in faith and in purity. (1 Tim. 4:12)

Possibly the most effective ministry an elder can give to his church is his own Christlikeness. It helps people grow in Christ if they can follow a concrete, tangible model, if they can see what it looks like to be a Christian. Plus, a Christlike elder is one who shepherds according to Christ's model, which of course affects every other activity undertaken, whether guarding, overseeing, or shepherding. According to these passages, an elder leads by his example, rather than "lording it over" those entrusted to his care.

I know elders who know well what they believe, but cannot express themselves in words very well. Nevertheless, they have outstanding ministries to their flock by means of their Christ-like lives. Their lives preach sermons.

S—Shepherd

Be *shepherds* of God's flock that is under your care. (1 Peter 5:2)

Be *shepherds* of the church of God, which he bought with his own blood. (Acts 20:28)

Shepherding, as we have seen, aptly describes the deepest motivation and orientation of the elder. Shepherding should characterize everything that the elder thinks, says, or does. But shepherding also refers to the concrete activity of looking after individual church members, monitoring their spiritual progress, and encouraging them on a person-to-person basis to grow in love and obedience to Christ. Of course, it would be impossible for an elder to have such an orientation without engaging in concrete shepherding activities. A shepherding program can't be equated with a shepherding orientation, yet some mechanism or structure must be in place to see to it that members get personal spiritual attention.

Much of the shepherding ministry can be delegated. A church can employ a single elder to do nothing but visitation. Elders can train members to minister to individuals under them. However, elders must also retain accountability. An elder must stay involved in shepherding enough that his members sense his spiritual care. He must also respond personally to those members who reject the delegated ministry.

There is no single, approved method to meet this goal. I have advised any number of approaches. Here are some concrete strategies:

- Set aside half of the monthly meeting of elders to consider and pray for members. (Obviously, this implies that you all have streamlined other matters! We'll talk about that in the next chapter.)
- Arrange for members to submit written prayer requests by dropping them in the offering plate. The session can rotate pairs of elders who will pray together for these requests before leaving the church building.
- Assign each family to an elder, to be part of his "flock." The elder should meet with his flock at least twice a year. At these meetings, he should help members understand that he desires to shepherd them in a way that transcends particular programs. He can build their confidence in him as a shepherd through this fellowship with them. He must also stress that members must exercise initiative in communicating with him.
- Each elder can organize his flock into subgroups, if his flock is large. Members in groups of ten to twenty can minister spiritually to each other, offering that crucial support and security that all of us require if we are to grow spiritually. Subgroups should meet regularly, and members in the group should consciously work at knowing and caring for each other outside of any structured program.

- Each elder should keep a log in which he records information and insights about each person in his flock. He can enter both formal visits and informal encounters. He can note the comments of anyone to whom he has delegated shepherding responsibilities. He can note his own assessment of that person. He can list that person's spiritual gifts and particular struggles. He can use this to prompt sensitive and informed intercession for that member.
- The elder must plan to visit with each family in his flock at least once a year.
- The elder ought to share in major events in a member's life. He can keep a record of these in his log: birthdays, anniversaries, an upcoming birth or graduation or surgery. He can phone or send a card, or find some other way to indicate his interest or concern.
- The elder can delegate much of this routine data-gathering and even visiting to a couple. I say a couple, because many positive benefits result from a husband-and-wife team ministering together. Also, it keeps one individual from figuring too prominently in the life of the flock. This arrangement can also afford a wonderful proving ground or apprenticeship to prospective elders.
- Don't forget the pastor and his family! At least two elders should be assigned to offer spiritual support and care to them.

I know one ruling elder in a church who, for several years, planned an early retirement so that he might minister part-time within his church as a shepherd. When he retired, the church hired him to vitalize an existing shepherding ministry. Now he spends his days shepherding and counseling, and teaches at a graduate school in the evenings. Part of his vision has been to shepherd; part of his vision has also been to help train younger elders, so that they can properly incorporate shepherding into their ministries.

There is not just one method for getting the job done. As you can guess, we can expect our shepherding ministry to take a shape that suits our particular gifts and needs.

The Complete Elder

Thus, God calls the elder to a fourfold ministry of guarding, overseeing, exemplifying Christ, and shepherding. Every job that an elder undertakes falls under one or more of these headings. Actively grouping his responsibilities along these lines enables an elder to streamline his job description, and it heightens his sense of calling to his ministry: "This is what God has called me to do; for these activities He equips me and empowers me."

Perhaps you feel overwhelmed by the task, especially by the prospect of shaping your whole life to fit the shepherd model, on top of everything else you have to do! Of course, by now we can see that the shepherd's heart in principle is not an add-on, but rather the fountainhead. Actualizing this outlook in individual elders and in the session as a whole should be a session's foremost commitment. Until elders think like shepherds, we have no right to expect that any activity in which they engage will bear the Chief Shepherd's stamp or the Spirit's blessing.

How can elders give their focus on shepherding the time and priority it demands? Elders can keep the ministry manageable by shortening the list of everything else they have to do. My strategy for church ministry will show how elders can be freed to tend to the basics, even as members exercise the Spirit's gifts for the common good.

The Senior Pastor: Elder Plus

A senior pastor occupies a unique position in the church. He is, on the one hand, (only) one ruling elder among many, equal in station and authority with them. On the other hand, he must also function as the leader of the church and thus of the other elders as well.

It takes liberal doses of the grace of God to blend these roles complementarily, as any seasoned pastor will testify. Erring in one direction or the other seems much easier. Overdoing the one-among-many role produces inadequate leadership; overdoing the one-over-many role leads to a dictatorial approach that is not good for the health of the church.

As one elder among many, he must exemplify the characteristics we have discussed in the last chapters. He must demonstrate biblical qualifications. He must continually grow in his leadership skills. He must think and minister like a shepherd. His ministry includes guarding, overseeing, exemplifying Christ, and shepherding.

But the pastor must exemplify each one of these characteristics in a special way. He must demonstrate biblical qualifications and maturity. The need for this is amplified by the fact that he regularly preaches the Word. It's as if he lives his life before his congregation as he preaches. He models Christianity. His life must match his message; his message must grow naturally out of his life. We cannot expect the Spirit to use anything less in the life of the congregation.

With regard to leadership, the pastor is the leader of leaders. With the public, the media in particular, he represents the entire church. Within the church, he leads the leaders; he also leads those who are led. God uses the pastor to lead the whole church in the vital worship that binds and motivates them. He enables the very meeting of the bride with the Bridegroom that heightens and satisfies our spiritual thirst. He proclaims God's Word with Spirit-given authority. He models the heart-felt worship that he seeks to develop in the congregation.

Because of his visibility and his unique role, he often becomes the lightning rod when difficulties arise. This comes with the territory, so to speak: pastors shouldn't expect it to be otherwise. They would do well to view these situations as special opportunities to witness and to demonstrate the love and grace of God. Catching the sparks affords the pastor access to the heart of the problem. He can thus apply his leadership skills—applying the Word to effect change—directly to the need.

The pastor should expect to exercise creativity in his leadership role. In fact, he should be a major source of new ideas within the church. I always teach my students never to enter a planning meeting with a blank piece of paper and the question, "Well, what shall we do?" The pastor should come with a list of creative ideas to propose. Note: I say propose, not impose! He can expect some ideas to remain unused, and others to be revised drastically. But he will have provoked others to think creatively, thereby leading by promoting change.

Because he preaches regularly, the pastor must be the church's visionary leader. A church has many leaders, both elders and others. One of them must present and interpret the church's vision, motivating all, leaders and followers alike, to buy into that vision. This facet of leadership belongs to the pastor. All the other leaders facilitate the vision's implementation.

Contrary to popular wisdom, however, it is not the pastor's personal vision that he espouses and to which he seeks to bend the church. It is the church's vision, and the pastor leads the charge in embracing and communicating it. We'll discuss this further in part 3. The two biblical directives, elder accountability and member initiative, shape my conclusions with regard to the church's vision. If a church has been asked to espouse an individual's personal vision, even if that individual is the pastor, the Spirit's gifts, as exercised by others, are being repressed.

Leadership, whether exercised by the pastor, the other elders, or anyone else, must always be open-ended and shepherdlike, creating an environment that encourages the initiative of those being led. We forget this and we sacrifice biblical health if we repress the Spirit's gifts. It might be easier to exercise greater control, and the "results" might be more apparently homogeneous and excellent. But we're after obedience to God, not results, and we have faith that obedience will produce results—results of God's choosing, not ours.

Nowhere in the biblical job description is the pastor a CEO. He is always a shepherd. Only through open-ended leadership can a pastor build the general perception that his ministry is one of shepherding a flock.

Questions for Discussion

1. How would you group your session's responsibilities under the four headings discussed in this chapter—guarding, overseeing, exemplifying Christ, and shepherding?
2. Are there some tasks that your session regularly performs which fall into none of these categories? Are

these tasks that other members of the church could perform? How could you delegate responsibility for them while maintaining oversight?

3. Are there some gaps in your list from question 1—areas that your session is overlooking (rather than overseeing)? What concrete steps can you take to rectify this?

Chapter 8 Ministry Centers: How Elders Can Be Accountable While Members Use Their Gifts

Healthy Practice #4: The church must have a mechanism for utilizing gifted member initiative while maintaining elder accountability.

We've approached the biblical concept of leadership from two directions now. In chapter 5, we discussed the two directives that must be balanced: elders must lead with accountability to God, and members must utilize their spiritual gifts. In chapters 6 and 7, we examined the Bible's concept of the elder as a shepherd, considering the outlook and the responsibilities that that involves.

Throughout these discussions, I've maintained that healthy, biblical leadership enhances rather than represses members' involvement. A strong leader does not do everything. Accountability does not require that. It is a mistake to confuse responsibility with accountability. It's almost as important to see what leadership isn't as to see what it is. The shepherd model reveals that biblical leadership consists of creating an optimal spiritual environment in which members can do what they do best, not doing it for them. To exercise oversight, others must be doing things that can be overseen. Godly authority is characterized, not by coercion, but by sacrificial care. All of these claims we've discussed along the way.

Now I wish to propose a mechanism that will enable us to carry all this out. For all our good intentions, sometimes we need a concrete procedure in order to live up to our ideals.

Who Is King of the Mountain?

One of those lessons that we learn early on in life, often at home or in school, is that every group of people has a "pecking order." One person is "king of the mountain," some are his lieutenants, others are at the bottom of the pecking order, and some seem to be outside of it altogether. Every group has what I call an authority infrastructure. That includes the church. Every church government exercises its authority in ways that amount to "authority highways." To continue the metaphor, these are the avenues by which we get things done.

Members can easily identify the authority infrastructure in their church. Newcomers come to recognize it over time, and we call this "getting to know the church"! On what basis do people reach their conclusions on this matter?

I have found that people subconsciously or consciously integrate their answers to the following questions in order to determine the church's authority infrastructure:

- Which individual or group more than any other generates the new ideas and statements of vision to be adopted?
- Which individual or group generally communicates these new ideas to the parties involved?
- Which individual or group operates the new ideas when they are implemented?

As you read these questions, you probably find yourself answering them with regard to your own church! I have developed a questionnaire to help me determine the perceived infrastructure of a church. A look at the results from fifty randomly chosen churches reveals two prevailing, detrimental perceptions:

One is that every new idea is generated by the pastor. This perception leads in turn to the conclusion that members' contributions have little significance—a direct contradiction of Scripture.

The other perception is that the elders operate all the ministries of the church, and ordinary members cannot serve the body in leadership roles of any importance. In such churches, elders simply don't have time to shepherd as they should, and the gifts, talents, and creativity of the people are ignored.

Members not initiating, elders not shepherding—these are the problems I have attacked in earlier chapters. Where such nonbiblical perceptions characterize a church, the unhealthy result fetters the powerful working of the Holy Spirit. The unhealthy state of affairs cannot persist indefinitely. Elders will burn out; members will remain spiritually stunted or will leave.

In some churches, on the other hand, the members cannot specify what is behind the programs or who is in charge. A church like this will soon divide into subgroups, and it will fail to exhibit unity when faced with a major decision. Occasionally, church members can recognize an official structure and believe that it conforms to Scripture, and yet they perceive that that structure is hopelessly ineffective. In this case, it may be that the official structure fails to match the real structure, or that the official structure's shell prevents both members and leaders from perceiving that no real structure is operative.

It may be that members' perceptions are erroneous. Often, sincere elders in no way intend to communicate what the members are perceiving. Unfortunately, in the eyes of the beholder, what is perceived is real. Members respond according to their perceptions.

The point is this: every church has an authority infrastructure. But not any old infrastructure allows a church to conform to the Bible's blueprint. Some positively thwart biblical health. Every church needs to develop and maintain an authority infrastructure that promotes health, allowing the Holy Spirit's multifaceted ministry to flourish.

A Closer Look at Decisions

In order to rectify an imbalanced situation, we need to begin by talking about decisions.

First, a church's ministry can be considered to be a composite of all the decisions it makes. A church's *ethos* is characterized by its decisions—what they are and who makes them.

Second, being involved in making decisions gives a person a sense of ownership. This is especially true today. What's more, people today want to be involved in decision making. Studies reveal that over 80 percent of the baby boomer generation wish to participate in an enterprise only if they can be significantly involved in decision making.

Third, there are three kinds of church decisions. Only the elders may make decisions concerning doctrine and government, such as how to apply a certain teaching to a new situation, or whether a prospective member's profession of faith is credible. Some decisions only the congregation can make, such as calling a new pastor or purchasing property. Then there are all the decisions that fall into neither of these categories.

The first two kinds of decisions may define the parameters of the church, but the third category, which is by far the largest, practically coincides with the life and ministry of the church! By the life of the church, I mean the organic, Spirit-bred, unprogrammable reality of God at work among us. By the ministry of the church, I mean the various programs and activities that we could list in the bulletin.

How can we encourage members to build relationships that offer support, comfort, and even restraint to one another? How can our church express concretely its confidence that the Holy Spirit has indeed gifted each one to serve significantly? How can I help Sally trust God in her parenting? How can our family befriend this new family? How do we organize the Sunday school? What shape does women's ministry take? What should the educational wing look like? How do we make visitors feel at home? Will a basketball ministry offer a way for young people to reach out to their friends? Which missionaries should we support, and how? All these matters fall in the third category of decisions.

Here is the key: this large third area of decision making offers ample opportunity for member leadership. Here individuals can utilize Spirit-given gifts and talents, make important contributions to the church, and acquire a fulfilling, growth-promoting sense of ownership. Meaningful involvement on this level knits loyalty to the body, promoting organic unity that stays intact through major, sometimes difficult decisions. When encouraged to exercise responsibility for both planning and implementation, members are usually set on fire for their church and their church's Lord. Also, in this kind of active service, future elders can mature.

Furthermore, as elders see how to allow others responsibility in this area while maintaining accountability, they can relinquish tremendous amounts of work to focus on the shepherding they were called to do.

Ministry Centers

I offer you my scheme of ministry centers as a mechanism which allows a church to achieve a healthy balance between member initiative and elder accountability, and which frees elders to minister as shepherds. You cannot read this plan in the pages of Scripture, but it is conformed to Scripture. I have had the privilege of seeing it work, transforming churches from frustrated, less-than-effective collections of individuals into joyful and well-honed instruments in God's kingdom. I remain personally committed to this scheme as the most effective way to develop a church that the Spirit will bless.

The concept of ministry centers fleshes out a single key insight: that it is possible for lines of accountability to remain intact even when significant, church-shaping decisions are being made by people for whom elders are accountable. This is the only way, as I see it, that we can do justice to both of Scripture's organizational directives (chapter 5). Use this insight as a criterion to evaluate the ministry centers scheme. It has shaped my proposal.

I propose that we organize all the activities of the church (in the third area of decisions) into ministry centers. In many churches, we already have something like them, called committees. I prefer the term *ministry center,* because it reminds us that the people involved are serving Christ in ministry, and because it doesn't lend itself as easily to a mistaken perception that the church's infrastructure is hierarchical. A ministry center, as I conceive it, may differ significantly from our usual conception of a committee. We tend to think of committees as impotent advisors or as worker bees—unless it is an executive committee, which "really gets things done." Significant, streamlined, vibrant ministry should characterize all these ministry centers. Ministry centers decentralize the ministry of the church, significantly involving members and freeing elders to shepherd, while not sacrificing their accountability. In this structure, members can use their gifts and talents, creativity and ingenuity. They can make important decisions, provide leadership, and do the work. Ministry centers, as tools of the Holy Spirit, enable members to own their church.

A typical list of ministry centers would include:

- worship and prayer
- Christian education
- member assimilation and support
- diaconal service
- small groups
- evangelism and missions
- Christian school
- facilities

A ministry center consists of an organized group of individuals endowed with significant authority to design and carry out certain church activities within certain parameters and in line with the church's overall vision. A ministry center team, under the leadership of its chairperson, sets specific objectives to be accomplished. The team determines the particular programs and activities that will constitute its ministry. It decides how the funds allotted to its ministry will be allocated. It sets its own standards for evaluating its efforts and implements a regular schedule of self-assessment.

The Ministry-Center Chairperson

The most significant stipulation about ministry centers is that they must be chaired by people who are not elders—male or female. We tend to think that committee chairmen should be elders, so that they can exercise proper oversight. Many churches assign elders to these key roles. But this common practice is mistaken and dangerous, as well as unnecessary for conscientious accountability.

When elders chair and organize these ministries, ordained leadership monopolizes power and inhibits members' spiritual contributions. Furthermore, elders involved at this level of church ministry cannot shepherd as they should, because they are too busy. This single stipulation frees elders to shepherd, and it opens the field for members to serve with a significant measure of authority.

Please note that both men and women can serve as chairpersons of ministry centers. In recent decades, feminism has provoked fresh and urgent questions about women in church leadership. In a church that restricts eldership to males and allows only elders to hold positions of significant leadership and authority, women can never hope to hold positions of significant leadership and authority. The gravity of this situation has been exacerbated by the mistaken notion that spiritual maturity should be identified with positions of spiritual leadership. A woman in this situation may feel barred from serving God in what is perceived to be a spiritually significant way.

However, my proposal to restrict elders from serving as chairpersons of ministry centers significantly lightens the frustration, while remaining faithful to Scripture. It breaks the airtight identification of elders with leadership and with spiritual significance. Others, male and female, for their own spiritual well-being and for the good of the church body, need to exercise their gifts strategically.

Accountability: Elders Interfacing with Ministry Centers

Elders interface with ministry centers in such a way that they can answer accountably for the centers' activities, but without doing the work themselves. In particular, the session must do three things:

1. The session must appoint or approve the chairperson for each ministry center. Obviously, this is best done on the basis of much prayer, research, consultation, and careful examination of any candidate.

2. The session must issue guidelines (and may also specify objectives) for each ministry center, delineating the boundaries of their operations. Guidelines enable a center to function freely within the framework of the church's doctrinal position and vision statement (see part 4), in harmony with the other centers. Significant initiative must still reside with each ministry center, or else we lose the chief value of this approach. The writing of guidelines also profits from prayer, research, and consultation especially with those likely to be involved in the ministry in question. Appendix A supplies details about writing and implementing these guidelines.

3. The session must oversee the work. The session will act as a resource for the chairperson, and it will act as a safeguard, with the authority to issue a veto, if necessary. I will spell this out concretely in the next section.

There is nothing to prevent an elder from helping out in a ministry. For example, he could teach a Sunday school class or sing in the choir.

Obviously, an arrangement like this, which grants significant initiative to those who are not elders, calls for elders to be prepared to do things differently from "the way we've always done it before"! Where elders exercise proper oversight, however, such originality and colaboring will prove inspiring to elders and members alike.

To make this work, we need one critical ingredient: trust. Elders must trust those who are not elders to do it. Submitting to the Holy Spirit includes treating with integrity the gifts He has given to individual members. A church develops from a group of individuals to a unified body of Christ as it exercises this kind of mutual trust. Elders set the tone by demonstrating their trust as they serve faithfully as overseers.

What's Involved in Elders Overseeing Ministry Centers

As I said, elders maintain accountability by appointing or approving chairpersons, specifying guidelines, and overseeing the centers' ministries. Let's see what oversight involves.

Normally, one elder oversees each ministry center. In larger churches, one elder may be called on to oversee two or three of them. Elders serving in this capacity I call "elder-overseers," or "E/Os." Oversight involves acting as a resource person, acting as a safeguard, and retaining veto power—the power to have the session veto a ministry center's proposal.

The E/O as resource. The ministry-center concept relies on and expects Spirit-given initiative to originate with members. Thus, the E/O's responsibility is primarily to encourage and enable the ministry center's chairperson.

The E/O *does not:*

- attend all the center's meetings, or even plan to do so.
- generate action plans, oversee schedules, etc.
- function as *de facto* head of the center.

The E/O *does:*

- pray regularly with the chairperson.
- receive regular updates about the center's action plans, personnel, finances, problems, progress, and major impending decisions.
- help the chairperson assess the relative urgency of competing demands.
- help the chairperson understand and apply guidelines, as necessary, especially when new situations arise.
- notify the chairperson of sessional decisions germane to the ministry.
- arrange the chairperson's occasional in-depth report to the session (the chairperson may request appearances more frequently).
- help publicize the center's work.
- keep the chairperson's "feet to the fire," gently but firmly holding the chairperson to his or her task of leading the ministry center to accomplish its objectives.

The E/O as safeguard. The ministry-center concept anticipates that chairpersons and participants will do new things, find creative approaches, and operate ministries in fresh ways.

As a resource person, the E/O encourages this. As a safeguard, the E/O insures that the center's initiatives fit within the specified guidelines.

In particular, the E/O:

- advises the chairperson of possible problems before things get too far along. For example, he may foresee a conflict with an existing program. Or he may recognize the potential for adverse results (such as a youth retreat with inadequate adult supervision).

- conducts occasional orientation workshops for members of the ministry center. These stress the church's vision and overall ministry, and explore the relationship between members' creativity and the session's guidelines.

- insures that the center's ministry is continually being evaluated. The E/O need not do this himself. He needs to be satisfied that it is being done effectively, and he needs to review the evaluations.

The E/O as veto. Actually, this role belongs to the session as a whole. An individual elder does not have the authority to veto something he deems to be too far from the church's vision, the ministry center's purpose, or the center's guidelines. But if his safeguarding has proved unsuccessful, he must summon the session to determine if a veto is necessary.

Usually a disparity of this degree indicates a personality problem. Before the session vetoes anything, pastoral or staff counseling may be advisable.

Ministry centers and the purse strings. What we agree to on paper does not always match what we do with our finances, and what we do with our finances usually qualifies as the bottom line! Here is the way to make our financial procedures match the ministry-center concept.

Responsibility for the church's ultimate financial viability resides with the elders. They approve and adopt an annual budget for the church. Each ministry center should have an individual line item in the budget. Each center will make specific financial decisions in the way that it makes every other decision: exercising its own initiative and utilizing its own leadership and creativity, with elders exercising oversight and veto power.

The elders must specify a uniform method of accounting to be employed by each ministry center. Both the overall budget and the standard accounting procedures are part of the guidelines for each ministry center (see appendix A).

Communication clinches accountability. In addition to the E/O acting as resource, safeguard, and veto "alarm," regular communication insures that the elders will oversee church ministries accountably. In addition to good communication between the chairperson and the E/O, the E/O in turn must reliably communicate with the session. Just as the E/O trusts the chairperson, so the session trusts the E/O. Regularly (monthly), the E/O needs to affirm that he has carried out his responsibilities and that he is satisfied that the ministry center is functioning well. Annually, the E/O should submit an in-depth report, including data sufficient for the session's own evaluations. The chairperson consults actively with the E/O as the latter writes his report. He also meets personally with the elders, once every two years, for a thorough review of the center's ministry.

Staff Members as Resources

Often a church is able to hire a staff member with a specific assignment to one of the church's ministries. Youth directors, music directors, and directors of Christian education fall in this category. So does the senior pastor! Among other things, he should be viewed as a key resource for the worship ministry team and also for the Christian education team.

How do paid staff members fit into the ministry-center scheme? The key word is *resource:* they are resources on which the center draws to accomplish its ministry. Ministry centers have other resources at their disposal. Facilities count as resources, and so do the manpower of the group and the members of the church. As we have seen, the elder/overseer also functions as a resource. All of these resources are available to the ministry center to utilize in the course of its ministry.

Paid staff members obviously turn out to be a ministry center's primary resource. A staff member suggests objectives and specific programs, feeding the ministry center's creativity in these areas. By virtue of his or her professional training, the staff member can be expected to have a good sense of the relative effectiveness or ineffectiveness of various strategies, and of their general cost. The ministry center draws on this expertise in making its choices.

A staff member can serve the center by fleshing out the details of specified programs. He or she will administer the programs and activities of the ministry center. This includes recruiting church members, as well as offering encouragement to all concerned with the ministry.

When a ministry center has access to a paid staff member, the staff member can be expected to administer the ministry's programs, rather than the chairperson doing this. The chairperson and the staff member must maintain communication. The staff member reports regularly to the ministry center, and the ministry center regularly evaluates the staff member's work.

Staff members are employed by the church (not by the ministry center), but they are employed to serve the ministry center. Thus, we must distinguish two lines of accountability for the staff member. As we've seen, in his or her administration of the ministry's programs, the staff member is regularly evaluated by the ministry center in terms of its own standards. But the staff member is also accountable to the senior pastor. In addition to his other roles, the senior pastor heads the church's staff, paid and unpaid. He exercises final authority in calling a staff member and in stipulating the terms of his or her call. The pastor oversees the staff person's life and relationship with the Lord, with family, with the congregation, and with the presbytery. He sees to it that staff members develop and use good leadership skills. The pastor must communicate the church's vision to his staff, continually monitoring their commitment to it and their implementation of it. The senior pastor assesses and acts on the ministry center's evaluative reports regarding the staff member. Thus, the ministry center guarantees the quality of its own ministry by holding a staff person accountable to carry out its responsibilities. The senior pastor guarantees the spiritual and ecclesiastical caliber of the staff person by overseeing his or her life and involvement. As part of the church's staff, staff members also contribute to the overall work of the church.

The key to this somewhat complex structure is *boundaries.* It takes some mental effort to shift our thinking about staff members and their relationship to their ministries. Staff members (and churches) often believe that they are the ones to adopt objectives as well as administer programs to meet them. But they must remember that the church is made up of people, not of staff. Actual decisions ought to be made by the people of the church. This calls for a sense of submission on the part of staff members, clear understanding of who answers to whom, and plenty of communication.

The staff member functions as a major resource, not as a final authority. The staff member administers programs; he or she does not adopt them. And the ministry center continually evaluates his or her ministry in light of the policies it has adopted. Separating these functions, which have traditionally been blurred, helps to keep the congregation involved. It offers clear lines of accountability, within which a staff person can minister with a freeing sense of his or her calling.

Ministry Centers Mean Ownership

I've seen the ministry-center approach transform a church. When people found that what they said was important to the life of the church, they began to own its ministry. Commitment and loyalty increased dramatically. One church of a hundred or so, prior to implementing a ministry-center approach, was facing a major crisis. Few members participated in church ministries, and a general perception prevailed that the leadership of the six elders was inadequate. The church was moving toward a rift that would have cost them almost half of their membership.

The elders committed themselves publicly to changing this. In particular, they committed themselves to reshape their ministry into one of shepherding, and they committed themselves to use people more significantly in ministry, using the ministry-center approach. God graciously allowed them to avert the crisis, and only a handful of people left the church. To church leaders, such a change may seem like losing power. In reality, it isn't losing ultimate authority; it is saying to the congregation, "We need you."

The ministry-center concept promises to resolve two difficulties that often prevent a church from being healthy. It allows both of the Bible's directives for church ministry to be met wholeheartedly: members can exercise Spirit-given gifts, initiative, and talent; elders can account properly to God for the church's life and ministry. It also offers a solution to the problem of how to free elders to shepherd God's flock in the way that God intended. A church with elders who shepherd and members who serve strategically is a very healthy church, one that can joyfully anticipate God's blessing.

Questions for Discussion

1. Describe the authority infrastructure of your church:
   a. Which individual or group more than any other generates the new ideas and statements of vision to be adopted?
   b. Which individual or group generally communicates these new ideas to the parties involved?
   c. Which individual or group operates the new ideas when they are implemented?
2. Name some of the decisions that make your church what it is, that do not need to be made by the session or ratified by congregational vote.
3. Brainstorm about how these decisions might be relegated to ministry centers. What ministry centers would your church have?

Part III

Implementing a Vision

Chapter 9 Your Vision: Uniquely You

Healthy Practice #5: The church must have a continually modified vision and plan, unique to that church body at that time and in that community, which focuses and implements its purpose and mission.

Now we need to talk, not about *the* church, but about *your* church.

We've talked about the wonder of the church, the bride of Christ, the body of Christ, the very presence of Christ on earth. I've shared with you my passion for the church, how I love that spiritual reality and long to see it moving toward that perfection that the Bridegroom has set about accomplishing. I've said that church health is this progression. (Note that health is the *progression*, not the *perfection!* It is frustrating, futile, and unbiblical to identify a healthy church with a perfected church. No church will be perfect this side of glory.) We've expressed the church's purpose and mission. We've examined several practices of a healthy church.

Now it is time to address an important subject hitherto only briefly mentioned. We need to talk about *your* church in its individuality. The biblically healthy practice of specifying a vision encourages a local church to capitalize on its Spirit-bestowed uniqueness. This practice of a healthy church is different from all others, for the end result of it is a local church that differs from just about every other local church.

All individual evangelical churches share the same purpose: to be the presence of Christ on earth, aspiring to His image, leading in His praise. All churches share the same mission: to carry out the Great Commission. All evangelicals share a need for shepherd leadership, for submission to Scripture's authority, and for utilizing vital worship to motivate spiritual growth. All benefit from a common passion to pursue God's ongoing work, as we shall see. And, yes, all churches benefit from specifying a vision. But were every local church to articulate one, we could expect few of their vision statements to read the same. Purpose and mission are universal. Health is a universal need and aspiration. But your vision is uniquely you.

A vision statement is a verbal expression of how your particular local congregation will carry out the universal purpose and mission of the church. If *purpose* explains why and *mission* explains what, *vision* explains how. A vision statement expresses the concrete way that your church, the spiritually gifted mix of believers whom God has brought together, with the resources that He is currently providing, in this particular community and time in history, will image and worship Christ and extend His kingdom.

To pursue this goal, we must look at Scripture. But we must also look at ourselves. We must exercise a great deal of faith. But that faith must capitalize on (rather than deny) the God-given resources and situation.

Finding 58th Street Presbyterian Church in Scripture

Do you find it difficult to believe that God has something unique in mind for your church? After all, isn't the idea to be *conformed* to Christ's image, pursuing a common goal? And if the Bible commands unity, how can there be any room for uniqueness? Wouldn't uniqueness be sinful?

And how can it be our church's business to study anything other than Scripture? How can it be godly to study ourselves? How could God be interested either in uniqueness or, to put it baldly, in us?

And how could we demonstrate faith of the mountain-moving sort if we expected our goals and commitments to reflect our own capacities and situation? After all, are we not to expect God to do the impossible?

A discussion of these questions would range far beyond the scope of this book. But they also suggest a mind-set that would keep a person or a congregation from grasping the import of this chapter. Perhaps you have at times been tempted to think this way. You would be in a large company!

Scripture diametrically opposes such a mind-set. Hear the words of the apostle Paul: "But in fact God has arranged the parts in the body, every one of them, just as he wanted them to be" (1 Cor. 12:18). In this passage, Paul has been developing the analogy of the body to explain spiritual gifts. The point is that the Holy Spirit gifts each member for the common good, and that it would be a mistake to think that everybody's gift is the same, or that we should all try to minister in exactly the same way. Of course, the end result is a unity, a *body;* but the whole point of the analogy is that unity leaves room for diversity.

God not only intends the diversity, but engineers it providentially. The Holy Spirit gives gifts, each with an individual's name on the tag. The tag does not say simply "Gift of Teaching" or "Gift of Mercy," but "Susan Bywater's Gift of Teaching" and "John Stolzfus's Gift of Mercy." God then bonds us together into a living organism in a particular time and place.

God does not just ordain the gifts and bind together the body. He also "foreordains whatsoever comes to pass," as the

Westminster Shorter Catechism, Q. 7, affirms. He also chooses the particular time and place. Why is your family in Mesquite, Texas? Why are you a part of the local church there? Why is that community the way it is, with its unique set of assets and liabilities? Why is all this taking place now? Although God does not reveal specific answers to these questions, we can be sure of the eternal significance of our individual situations.

The Holy Spirit doesn't simply applaud uniqueness. The circumstances and the mix of believers in which we find ourselves isn't simply a chance affair that we attempt to surmount. God ordained the unique mix that is your church, and He ordained its context.

The next step is to recognize that, in order to figure out God's will for your church, we need to look beyond Scripture. The Spirit works actively, not only in connection with the words of Scripture, but also in connection with the gifts and the body dynamic of your church. To keep in step with the Spirit, we must take these gifts and this dynamic seriously. God has arranged them in your church body just as He intended them to be. To assess gifts, resources, interrelationships, and even demographics, which we have to do to write a vision statement, is therefore very much a spiritual exercise. To overlook this is to offend the Holy Spirit. To overlook it is also to miss out on an exciting dimension of healthy church life.

Treating individual members' spiritual gifts with integrity is one of the two biblical directives that must be balanced. The other directive, accountable shepherd oversight, must enhance rather than diminish the use of members' gifts. In part 2, we said that shepherd leadership balances these two directives. I have proposed establishing ministry centers as a mechanism to carry it off. In this last section, we meet a second implication of treating members' gifts with integrity. Gifts, along with resources and the situation, uniquely characterize each congregation and must be factored in as that body thinks seriously about how to fulfill its purpose and mission. In other words, these providential and spiritually arranged aspects significantly shape our church's vision.

What a Vision Is and What It Isn't

A vision statement, as I said, expresses concretely how a church will fulfill its purpose and mission. To help you understand more clearly what I have in mind, let me distinguish the healthy goal from common misconceptions.

Every church, whether it has thought about it or not, already has a vision! A vision is like a person's character or personality—something you have even when you aren't trying to have one. All the choices our church makes and all the activities we carry out suggest a style, an unspecified something that we aim for. So when I implore you to specify a vision, I am not asking you to develop something new. Rather, I'm asking you to articulate what has been shaping you without your knowing it. And as you subject your vision to this scrutiny, I'll ask you to revise it regularly in light of certain factors and strive to minister consciously in terms of it.

Many churches simply haven't thought about their vision. If they consider adding a program, they often don't even have a rationale for doing so. But a church whose vision has not been consciously specified and used as a rationale for its ministry is essentially a church without a rudder.

If some churches specified their working goal, it would simply be to maintain the programs already in place. Perhaps their vision is, "We want to be comfortable; don't rock the boat"! They want to hear the gospel, though not in a way that challenges their existence to the core (but is that really the gospel of the Lord Jesus Christ?). They want to have friends and good fellowship, and they want to lead their own lives. In a church such as this, the internal dynamic of friendliness is high, but there is no deeper dynamic of unity in the cause of the gospel.

Many such churches have missed out on the benefits of articulating a vision because they do not realize that it is a spiritual, biblical endeavor. Others are not oriented to the task. Others resist anything that questions the status quo. It takes God-given courage to embrace change and growth. There is a close connection between pursuing church health and hammering out a vision. Both require a desire to mature. In fact, as we'll see, taking steps toward church health must be included in a church's vision statement and action plans.

Many churches have made the effort to write a vision statement. Believe me, any effort pays big dividends! But among these churches, there are three common misconceptions that lessen the value of the result.

Some churches have ended up simply restating the church's universal mission (the Great Commission) or its universal purpose. To do that is in effect to specify the what and the why without talking concretely about the how. It is to attend to the Word without attending to the Spirit's unique gifts to a particular congregation. Often this occurs because they haven't understood their spiritual gifts or realized that they suggest a concrete application of the church's universal purpose and mission. We can think of the church's universal purpose as its *Founder's vision;* we must articulate what we might call the *followers' vision.* If this misconception describes your church's vision, take heart: your task is partially completed, and what you read here will point the way to finishing it.

Some churches, and certain writers on the subject, believe that a church's vision is the pastor's or the session's brainchild.[1] On this view, a vision can even be thought of as something bordering on a supernatural revelation. Or the pastor's vision may be his personal, concrete message that he intends to live out through his church. Either way, the congregation's role is simply to get on board. Some mistakenly believe that this approach is essential if leaders are to be held accountable for their flock. Some churches even expect a congregation to "own" this vision, not recognizing the insensitivity and impropriety of this demand. But a vision is not automatically transferable from the pastor to the people.

A vision specified by the leadership denies that the Spirit deals with or through anybody in the body besides the leaders. That contradicts the plain teaching of 1 Corinthians 12. Plus, it exposes the church to serious dangers. It's hard for the congregation to feel significant apart from the leadership. If the pastor's vision alone counts, the morale and the participation of the members may well decline.

Suppose a member with leadership and even pastoral potential fails to agree with or fit in with the pastor's vision. How will his contribution be appreciated? What happens is that a pastor gathers around him those who agree with his vision. Anyone disagreeing with it would feel tempted to go in search of another church body, in which he or she stood a chance to be significantly involved.

And what if the pastor leaves? What happens to the church and its vision? A destructive vacuum can follow in the wake of such a departure.

And finally, what if the pastor is wrong about the vision? How would we (or he) know? Who would judge him? How could anyone question the vision without being branded as disobeying God or contesting authority? How could we protect the church from the damage caused by an excessively powerful but mistaken leader?

Thus, I believe that it is unbiblical and dangerous to say that the pastor or the leadership originates the vision. Rather, the vision must be the *church's* vision.

Can God use a church whose vision has been specified by the pastor? Of course! As I said before, any effort to bring the church's life and ministry into line with a vision will have a positive effect. Also, God seems to be in the business of putting his treasure in broken pots, using our misguided, sin-flawed attempts for His glory—"to show that this all-surpassing power is from God and not from us" (2 Cor. 4:7). But this verse should never be used to deny the need for improvement! Positive results from specifying a vision should not automatically be taken to mean that we have arrived spiritually. We must always expect further growth, and in that growth we must seek to understand Scripture's standard more profoundly and model it more precisely.

I know a church whose vision, succinctly stated, is to be a relational church in a contemporary mold. This is a fine vision, and a fine statement of it. God has blessed this church's self-conscious shift to this approach, which was made a few years ago. However, the vision originated with the pastor. He knows exactly where he is going, and holds to it with an iron grip. The people have not been involved in developing a vision among themselves, nor in offering ongoing evaluation and revision.

What has happened is that the pastor has gradually insulated himself with elders who think similarly. When other men who don't go along with the vision—biblically qualified men with leadership skills—have been nominated for ordination, these nominations don't even get to the floor. What has happened to these aspiring shepherds who do not fit the pastor's vision? They have given up and quit. An inbred situation is developing, as sources of fresh fertilization, so to speak, are continually ruled out of court.

Is it right for a session to bar names from being nominated? I think not. Nothing in Scripture says that an elder must promise to abide by a certain vision, in the way that he must promise to abide by a certain doctrine and government. For a session to stipulate this, formally or informally, is to raise vision to the status of doctrine and government. In effect, it is to impose an extrabiblical standard, to add to Scripture.

Now, it would be quite appropriate for a prospective elder to remove himself from consideration if he is aware of his own disharmony with the prevailing approach. But if such a person, already a member of the church, has been nominated, then the church really should consider whether God wants it to modify its vision.

If your church's vision originates with the people, rather than with the pastor, two things should happen. First, your people should stick with you. Second, your pastor, along with everybody else, should continue to grow as the vision grows.

A third misconception about vision statements is that once they are specified, they apply for all time. A church could easily think this way if its vision statement had an aura of revelation to the pastor or the session. But other factors can also lead people to believe that their vision applies forever, not the least being that after all the work it took to articulate one, it would be a shame if it didn't last a long time!

But to think this way might well lead to problems some years on. The unique God-ordained aspects of your church—the mix of spiritual gifts, the intangible dynamics that bind you together, your facilities and resources, your clientele, and your geographical and temporal location—continually change. God has brought us five new families. Two key elders have been transferred. There's been a baby explosion. God has matured us spiritually, and we're ready for fresh challenges. The Advent candles burned down the sanctuary. The number of divorces in our community has tripled. General Motors is building a plant that will revive the economy in our town. We've moved to the suburbs. The student body of the local university now represents a third of our city's population; they're mostly homosexual and postmodern. And, yes, the ideas of the 1990s are giving way to the ideas of the third millennium.

Obviously, the concrete way our church images Christ and extends His influence must continually be revised. It must be revised, not because we didn't get it right before (though maybe we didn't), and not because we were spiritually deficient (though maybe we were), and not because we have to exercise some pagan marketing savvy if we are to keep our sacred ship afloat (the problem here is the false dichotomy). We state the vision in the first place, and we revise it every few years, because Scripture directs us to take these constantly changing elements seriously, as ordained by God Himself. We expect to redo it because we mature through ongoing self-evaluation. If the self-evaluation stops, maturing will stop, too. We need to think of the vision as a revisable document, finally, because it is inherently a human document, subject in the best of circumstances to our finitude and sin. Would it not be sacrilegious to deem it immune to criticism or improvement?

Write a vision statement. Unpack it in an action plan. Implement your plans. But expect to do it again in three to five years—and again, and again. This is what it means to grow and to be healthy.

Focusing Your Vision

Here is a strategy to follow to focus your vision, one that remains consistent with Scripture's stipulations about treating members' gifts with integrity and about accountable shepherd oversight, and one that involves a realistic assessment of changing factors.

This assessment process will result in a vision statement that can in turn shape a concrete plan of action that addresses every aspect of church life and ministry. A vision statement has two parts. One is a short paragraph describing your church's unique application of the church's universal purpose and mission. Often this paragraph can be reduced to a pithy motto, the kind of thing you put on your bulletin, on your letterhead, and on the lips of every member and visitor.

The second part is the vision explanation. It takes each phrase of the vision statement and explains its implications for this congregation in its present circumstances. It begins to apply the vision as you develop action plans. In the next chapter, we'll speak in more detail about action plans.

The important result, the wonderful benefit, is that everyone knows what the church is about and how each part contributes to the overall focus. Everyone's faith is stretched to meet it; everyone senses the unity of single-mindedness and enjoys the motivation it brings. And even the community will have a clearer sense of the church's goal and contribution.

You can expect to take several months to draft a vision statement. The process will involve just about everyone in the church in some measure. And, as I said, you need to keep in mind that you'll undergo the whole process again in several years.

Appoint a task force. A vision statement task force will spearhead the process. This group, I suggest, should consist of the pastor and two members who are neither elders, deacons, nor staff. They will orchestrate the process of collecting information and evaluating it, and they will write up to five different possible vision statements that reflect that information, from which eventually one statement will be selected.

All members of the task force must demonstrate a firm commitment to change toward corporate spiritual maturity, a commitment that will resist the temptation to give in to others' stubbornness and fear. If necessary, these members will also serve as the agents of change, taking action to help others embrace fresh challenges in spiritual growth.

They must pray and exercise faith in dramatic proportions. Each day should find them praying that God will lead and that He will stretch their faith. And they must grow in exercising what I call "stretched faith." If you think of "no faith" as an unwillingness to dream about or try anything new, and you think of "insane faith" as wishing to attempt things that take no account of our unique set of gifts, resources, and situation, then "stretched faith" will fall in between these two extremes. Stretched faith will involve dreaming about the possibilities (perhaps as opposed to insane faith's dreaming about the impossibilities). It will be dreaming in terms of the special Spirit-endowed aspects of the church. It will involve taking the risk that the Lord Jesus likens to investing the talents in the parable of the ten minas (Luke 19:11–27). The ultimate goal of the task force is to capture such stretched faith while recognizing the realities facing the church.

Given his particular gifts, passion, and role in church life, it is likely that the pastor will insure that prayer and stretched faith characterize the task force's activity. He will be directly responsible for this, in addition to helping in every facet of the work of the task force.

Involve the congregation. The process of formulating or revising a vision will have as its central activity collecting information about the church's current gifts, dynamics, resources, and situation. The task force must involve the congregation in collecting information. Without the congregation's broad involvement, the data gathered will not adequately represent the unique aspects of the church. What's more, this will allow the church to be serious about spiritual gifts. Also, it will help everybody to own and support the process. Finally, it will provoke just the kind of self-evaluation that leads to growth. Sometimes it is fun and sometimes it is painful, but without it, no growth can occur.

How do you go about this? One good way is to send out questionnaires. Another way is to hold small-group discussions and brainstorm. Or you can conduct family interviews. Whatever method you use, delegate data gathering to key members of the congregation. Gathering this information should take about three months.

Collect the facts. The kind of information you're looking for falls into four basic categories: unique aspects of the body; unique needs of the geographic area; church resources, programs, and activities; and existing dynamics. Information will include concrete details such as the level of giving, but it will also include general perceptions of the current state of affairs. Remember, people's perceptions of reality are often more important than the way things actually are!

Data will also have to be assessed. Is our church functioning adequately in this area? Is there potential for improvement or growth?

Unique aspects of the body. Here we get a sense of how the Holy Spirit has gifted our members and our congregation to worship and serve Him. This information can also shape our sense of how He intends to use us and cause us to grow during the next few years. Try to answer these questions:

- What does the congregation perceive to be the church's four greatest strengths? How does it rank them from strongest to weakest?
- How satisfied are members with this or that aspect of the life and ministry of the church?
- What do they expect or anticipate regarding the church's life and ministry?
- What kinds of spiritual gifts have we already identified among the congregation? Who is really good at what, and who loves what they do and sees God blessing it? Remember that someone may not recognize his own spiritual gifts as well as those whose lives he touches may recognize them! It's useful to allow people to point out one another's gifts.
- What kinds of ministries do people sense that the Spirit is drawing them to pursue? Do these match up with existing ministries of the church?
- Which people demonstrate as yet untapped potential for leadership?

The church's unique surroundings. The task force should identify the geographic area that it believes the church should try to influence. Of course, we all share a mission to reach the entire world! But we must recognize that God has uniquely and strategically positioned our church to reach one specific area of the world. Try to answer these questions:

- What lifestyles characterize the population in our area? In addition to culling your own perceptions, you could research government census records or employ a professional demographer.
- What values, ideas, and needs characterize people in this area?
- What are the major features of our community (for example, a university, a hospital, a large shopping mall, a military base, an industrial park)?
- How do the above characteristics afford the church unique opportunities to witness or to extend mercy?

Existing resources, programs, and activities. This study will help us to assess the programs, manpower, finances, facilities, and staff with which we currently work. Answer the following questions:

- What are all of our church's programs and activities? Who is the key individual responsible for each?
- On the basis of the congregation's internal demographics for the past three years, what trends and emphases characterize attendance, financial support, and percentage of members doing the majority of the work of the church? Supply as much concrete data and as many actual names as you can.
- What facilities does the church have available? These include buildings, grounds, access to city-owned facilities, members' property that is used regularly for church purposes, the manse, vans, parking areas, and paid staff (see chapter 8).
- In light of your answers to these questions, how well is the church currently using its resources? Do we

utilize our property as effectively as we can? Does our congregation tithe faithfully, or can this be improved? Does the church benefit from a majority of members sharing responsibilities, or can this be improved? Do the type and number of staff we employ correlate with our current needs and spiritual ambitions, or should this be adjusted?

The church's present dynamics. What I have in mind by "dynamics" are the often intangible ways we relate to one another within the body, along with the factors that shape these interrelationships. Try to answer these questions:

- How does this church's past heritage shape the way we do things now? For example, do we still cherish our allegiance to the Confederacy? Did our church get put on the map because our forefathers engaged in some political or doctrinal battle that is no longer a burning issue?

- What situations, recent or current, affect our interrelationships? For example, do certain families still distance themselves from the leadership because of last year's quarrel over the public discipline of one of their number?

- What four things does the congregation generally perceive could be strengthened (including pastor's and elders' ministries), and how do these rank in importance?

- What is the likely response to attempts to remedy matters that are perceived to need strengthening?

- How does the congregation perceive that authority is used in the church, and by whom?

- How is this authority passed along? Who has the ideas? Who facilitates their implementation? By what means?
- How friendly are members toward some or all of the congregation? Toward visitors?
- How unified or bonded is the congregation? Is this bonding merely social, or is it also spiritual?
- How conformed is the congregation to the characteristics of a healthy church? Do elders function as shepherds? Does worship motivate growth? Have we balanced accountable oversight with treating individual gifts with integrity? Is the Bible our hallmark both in name and in reality?

By the time your church gathers this information, you will know just about all there is to know about your church! But good stewardship requires familiarity with the resources. Once you are experts on the current state of affairs, you will be in the best position to estimate God's design for your current congregation and to recommend a vision. Plus, if everybody is included in the process, your congregation will probably be intensely engaged in considering these issues and eager to formulate a vision statement.

It's best to record all the collected data and their assessment in a document, which is available for all to read. This will insure that everybody feels included.

Draft the vision statement. The task force next discusses this data, drawing out every implication and making every assessment that they believe to be germane to forging a vision statement. They will have to reconcile some things. For example, our community may need a university campus ministry to intellectuals, but our congregation may have few college graduates in it. The latter circumstance may suggest the inadvisability of pursuing a campus outreach at the present time, but may indicate the need to pray about God's equipping for the future. It may suggest a ministry of mercy to students, perhaps foreign students, rather than an invitation to exchange ideas. The process will also involve weighting various aspects of the church's life and ministry. Does God want us to address a certain weakness directly, or does He want us to focus our efforts elsewhere? Obviously, this calls for spiritual wisdom and discernment, and it calls for stretched faith. It demands that we saturate the effort with prayer.

The next step is to write up to five proposals for how the church should attempt to express Christ's presence and influence in this community over the next few years. From these proposals, the task force will prayerfully select one to be the church's vision statement. The vision statement must reflect a balance of two factors, both divine in origin: on the one hand, it must reflect stretched faith—a willingness to trust God to demonstrate His power in and through us by leading us to ever greater heights of spiritual growth and ministry; on the other hand, it must reflect the gifts, resources, and situation that He has already provided.

The task force will then draft a two- to three-paragraph vision statement and a pithy motto. It will also write a concrete explanation of each phrase of the vision statement—what I have called the vision explanation. This document should represent the culmination of your church's discussion.

Take it to the elders. The task force will then present the vision statement, along with all supporting evidence, to the session. Its proposals will not come as any surprise to the elders, if the congregation has been as fully involved as I have urged.

Normally, the session will accept this work, offering minor feedback for the purpose of fine-tuning.

The session's critical role consists of formally adopting the vision statement and then recommending it to the congregation for approval.

The elders must do this, not the task force. The reason for this is that the church's leadership must demonstrate its willingness to buy into the vision, to support it, to live and minister in terms of it, to lead in its actualization.

As we shall see next, elders will also shepherd the congregation in order to enable them to comprehend the implications of the vision, and to encourage them to embrace it. Finally, they will hold a congregational meeting for its adoption.

Take it to the congregation. Another distinctive feature of this approach is that the vision statement will be formally adopted by the congregation's vote. This is quite consistent with all that I have said so far. However, churches that misconceive of the vision as being the pastor's or the session's, or who believe the vision to be only a restatement of the Great Commission, will fail to grasp the propriety and the importance of the congregation voting to adopt it.

The session must do more than simply hold a parliamentary meeting. It must first make significant efforts at communication. The elders must present the vision in oral and written form, on multiple occasions, to individuals and families and groups, allowing for plenty of discussion. The elders must make sure that members understand the vision's implications, and, in the process of communicating its implications, they should inspire and motivate compliance. Only when everyone understands the vision should a meeting be called to adopt it. A vote is a commitment to support the vision.

Taking the vision to the congregation must proceed in the context of much prayer on everyone's part, along with mutual encouragement to stretched faith, and preferably in the company of a shepherd. Any vision worth its salt will call for a fresh self-evaluation, for change, for pursuit of spiritual goals just beyond our current levels, for more or different involvement in service, and for greater commitment. Our frail hearts, apart from divine intervention, falter at the thought. Only prayer, stretched faith, and the encouragement of a spiritual leader and other people with enable us to rise to the challenge.

An Example

Let me briefly describe one local church and show you their vision statement. This church of about 150 people, in the suburbs of a fairly large city, has six elders, including the pastor. It has its own building, but recognizes that the building is no longer adequate. Its family mix includes almost all age groups, with the greatest number being between thirty and forty-five years of age. The city is growing. The majority of members are white-collar professionals. People in the community, it was revealed, feel that their greatest needs include good family relationships and guidance parenting teens in today's culture. The church's pastor is deeply appreciated as a Bible teacher who expounds the Bible in the context of life today. The church appears to be basically healthy, its greatest needs being to improve communication and shepherding.

The church adopted a vision statement that would emphasize developing the ministries of the church, especially the preaching and teaching of the pastor, into a center known to provide answers for contemporary life through powerful biblical preaching and teaching. In addition to shaping the pastor's ministry, this vision particularly impacts the church's ministry to youth and Christian education. But it also bears on the entire life and ministry of the church, and on every individual member. Here is their focus:

> The XYZ Church seeks to be a worshiping body of believers committed to growing into a regional center for gracious biblical teaching.

They selected this pithy maxim:

> XYZ Church: Centered on the Bible as Life for Contemporary Living

They expressed the concrete implications of the vision statement in the following vision explanation:

> The concept of "worshiping body" means that XYZ Church is committed to:
>
> - place worship as the primary motivator of the life and ministry of the church;
> - seek constantly to worship God in a vital way, with the consequent commitment to evaluate regularly its vitality and apply the lessons learned so that the worshipers know they have been in the presence of the Living God.
>
> The concept of "growing into a regional center" means to be committed to using the unique potential of the people and location of XYZ Church to enable the congregation as well as many other Christians and churches

(in the northern area of the city) to become committed to the Bible as the final rule of faith and life.

The concept of "gracious" means that the congregation is committed to maintain throughout its life and ministry the testimony that it is a people of Christian friendliness and concern.

The concept of "biblical teaching" means that the teaching involved in growing into a regional center will place the Reformed Faith as the system of doctrine of the Bible so that it becomes the effective foundation for living.

In addition, proposals for increasing the health of XYZ church have been made a specific part of the Action Plan Outlines and have been important dynamics affecting the Vision Statement itself.

Also built into the Vision Statement, again based heavily on external demographics, is the commitment to grow to approximately 500 and always to be in the process of preparing to plant daughter churches.

Implementing Your Vision

All of these efforts to articulate a vision, of course, do not grind to a halt once the vision is adopted. The vision must be implemented. This will call for more prayer and more faith-stretching creativity. The goal will be to apply the vision to every aspect of the life and ministry of the church, spelling out its concrete implications for each, and bringing the actual state of affairs into conformity with these implications. I have conceived of this process as writing an action plan. We'll talk about this in the next chapter.

It's great for a church to be aware of its awesome significance according to Scripture. It's wonderful for it to know its universal purpose and mission, the why and the what that make it like every other church. But a church that knows these things and hasn't undertaken to forge a concrete vision will to that extent be incomplete. It won't have the whole story, for it will not know itself and what the Holy Spirit has particularly in mind for its ministry.

Articulating a vision can be an arduous process. But so is aerobic exercise! No pain, no gain, we say, and we thereby affirm also that if there is pain, there will definitely be gain. This tool can be a tremendous impetus for spiritual growth, both individually and corporately. Only one thing will deter its effectiveness: unwillingness to change and grow.

I recall sadly an older church in a city, once having a membership of 400 to 500, whose members were unwilling to change. Their large session said to me, "We have all these rooms in our church; why don't people come?" The reality of the situation was that the surrounding neighborhood had changed so much that nobody concerned about safety would go there after 4 p.m. without an escort.

I suggested that they gut the building and reshape it, that they tap local social agencies for information in order to discover the concrete needs of people living nearby, and that the church find a way to become necessary to the community as a resource for everyday life, all in the name of the gospel. I suggested that they start a lunch outreach to businessmen. I suggested that they make Sunday worship an afternoon service to accommodate elderly traditionalists.

The church did not respond to this challenge to change. This kind of built-in entrenchment, apart from the powerful working of the Holy Spirit, offers very little hope for a breakthrough.

May God enable your congregation to take the risk, to lay hold of His resurrection power, to dream big, and to experience the palpable results of forging a vision.

Questions for Discussion

1. Has your church articulated a vision statement?
2. If it has, did the vision statement originate with the pastor, the session, or the congregation?
3. If it has not articulated a vision statement, what unexpressed vision do you think is operating to shape the life and ministry of your church—what does your church generally think of itself as being and doing and striving for?
4. Brainstorm briefly about whatever portion of this list you have time for:
   - the unique aspects of your church
   - its greatest strengths
   - member satisfaction
   - spiritual gifts
   - potential leadership
   - unique needs and opportunities of the church's surroundings
   - values and needs
   - major features
   - opportunities for ministry
   - existing resources, programs, and activities
   - programs

- finances and membership
- facilities
- how effectively these are being used
- existing dynamics
- historical background which still influences life and ministry
- relationships between people
- areas that need strengthening
- authority infrastructure
- friendliness to visitors
- unity
- practices of a healthy church

5. In light of this chapter, what steps would be good for your church to take? How and when will you get started?

Chapter 10 Writing Action Plans

Were you to have carried out the entire process of writing a vision statement, as set forth in the last chapter, without any awareness of the contents of this chapter, you might be tempted to think that you were now faced with an equally large task. How disheartening that would be! However, as you'll see quickly, writing action plans flows naturally from writing a vision statement; the two form a seamless whole.

Had you simply written a vision statement following my guidelines, you would have soon discovered that in the process you had already taken great strides toward preparing action plans. You've prayed, you've stretched your faith through the Holy Spirit's empowering, you've accepted the challenge to change, you've discovered a lot of neat ideas in the course of your collective brainstorming. And if, for some reason, you were now prevented from working out that vision in the nitty-gritty of church life, you would find that incredibly frustrating.

Vision and action plan are inseparable. A vision statement without an action plan is useless. A church that makes plans in the absence of an overarching vision will similarly experience futility and disunity. Unfortunately, each of these scenarios occurs frequently.

This chapter will not add significantly to the efforts prescribed in chapter 9. The sweeping, synthetic part is behind you;

this is the practical, detailed part. You should feel as if you've crested the mountain and are coasting down the other side.

Action Plans: What and Why

An action plan is your church's concrete description of how you intend to implement your fresh vision. It specifies intended changes and implications for the organic life of the church, for the ministries of the church, for the authority infrastructure of the church, for the church's staff, and for its facilities.

Obviously, the key question that must be answered is this: what does your fresh vision statement imply concretely for the life, ministries, and infrastructure of your church? What does it imply for your overall slate of activities, your membership involvement, and your budget? What does it imply for your facilities? What additions will you have to make to your staff? And what do you envision the results being for your church's life—what percentage increase in attendance, giving, involvement, conversions, and contacts in the community?

When you've finished your action plan, you will know the following for each proposed change: whom you will need, how much it will cost, by what date it will be fully implemented, and what you believe will result. You will also be able to summarize this information. You will be able to generate a timeline to guide the implementation of the entire vision. You will be able to estimate the overall manpower you will need to implement the vision—what persons, by what time, and how each will be utilized. You will be able to estimate the cost, generating a budget that indicates how much you need, by what time.

Planning and implementation must be pursued with a view toward actualizing a single, overarching vision. The vision serves as a guiding light, effecting unity, offering clear guidance. How could we move forward without it? The goal for which we're shooting always remains clear.

Your action plan will have a twofold purpose. Its primary purpose will be to apply your vision. But you should also utilize this vision-to-action process to address any health concerns of the sort raised by this book. In effect, specifying a vision and an action plan gives you a concrete mechanism for change—for any change a church needs to make.

Remember, the process ought to be repeated every three to five years, for God is ever at work, changing us, reshaping the needs and opportunities. A span of three to five years allows time for ongoing evaluation of the kind that leads to prayerful, premeditated change. In that time frame, it may become apparent, for example, that our children and their friends qualify now more for youth ministry than for summer Bible school, that a new facility would offer fresh opportunities for outreach, that an influx of single parents calls for extended family support, and that the shutdown of a nearby plant suggests the need for a food pantry or a career service.

I distinguish between an action plan and action plan outlines. The action plan is the overall plan. It is a single document that includes all the individual changes as well as the overall fitting together of these individual efforts. The action plan describes how the overarching vision will be implemented, Lord willing. It shows each part, and it also shows how all the parts will fit together. An action plan outline is a plan for an individual program or activity, one outline per program or activity. An action plan outline will be written for any program or activity being introduced or modified. One does not need to be written for current programs or activities that already dovetail with the church's fresh vision statement. All the action plan outlines will be brought together to generate the church's action plan.

Do you also see that this stage must be bathed in prayer, and that stretched faith will be needed if we are to move forward in Christ? It takes as much courage to spell out the implications of a vision as it takes to formulate it in the first place—and perhaps more!

It is important to have an action plan because apart from it you're likely to get precious little action—or you're likely to get actions other than the ones you'd like! Positively stated, an action plan, because it is so concrete, can move people to serve and grow to a measure unattainable without it. The action plan puts feet on the vision.

I remember the time when God drove home to me the importance of having a plan of action. I received a call from the pastor of one of our mission churches in Florida. He told me that the church was voting that weekend to leave the denomination! The church, many of whose members were retired, had organized and built their building using denominational funds; now the organizing pastor was leading them to another denomination!

I canceled my engagements and flew directly to Florida. I asked them for an opportunity to speak to the issue. I got in touch with a man whom I knew to be available to serve as pastor, and who had a proven gift for working with older people. I secured from him an offer to pastor that church if the church was willing.

A tragic event on Saturday night—a member was killed in an automobile accident on the highway in front of the church—postponed the meeting until Sunday morning and heightened the soberness of the occasion. We met for twenty minutes of worship, and then I offered them a plan. My proposal included a concrete offer with respect to manpower and finances, and I offered a concrete timeframe in which this would occur.

When the church voted on the question of leaving, 52 percent of the congregation voted to stay! Without the plan, they would have voted the other way. Proposing concrete plans always addresses the need more effectively.

Hammering It Out

The action plan process starts where the vision process leaves off. The transition is seamless.

After a vision statement has been adopted by a congregation, the next step is to think about what changes the church ought to make in order to bring itself into line with its new vision. Consider, for example, the church whose vision statement we looked at in detail: they felt that God was leading them to think of themselves as a regional center for biblical teaching. They wanted to promote the pastor's pulpit ministry. Concretely, this might entail media advertisement, a pastor's column in the newspaper, perhaps a radio program, additional staff to enable the pastor to focus on preaching and teaching, a study leave for the pastor, special conferences, etc. Choosing between such alternatives is what the action plan is all about.

Here are the steps that must be taken:

- Decide, in light of the vision and with a view to church health, what areas must be modified.
- Outline concrete plans to address these needs.
- Reconcile these outlines into a single, overarching plan.
- Implement this action plan.

Let's look at each of these in turn.

Deciding what areas to modify. By the time the vision-writing process is complete, everybody in the church ought to have a good idea of what adjustments will need to be made to bring the church into line with its fresh vision. Somebody needs to specify formally in writing what these areas are. The vision task force would be a good group to prepare the document. But whoever does it, they must formally recommend to the session the areas to be addressed. As much congregational input as possible at this point will maintain everybody's involvement and ownership. Remember, the congregation has just voted to adopt the vision. Like any new owners, they now have a vested interest in developments. Capitalize on this vested interest. Doing so will contribute directly to the spiritual health of your church.

Every aspect of the church must prayerfully be examined in light of the fresh vision. Here you may think in terms of the distinctions specified in chapter 2 (as in my analogy): the church's life—its heart; the church's ministries—its flesh; the church's authority infrastructure—its skeleton. Staff and facilities, which are secondary aspects that I likened to clothing, will automatically be scrutinized as part of these larger aspects.

Consider your church's life, that intangible but essential spiritual vibrancy. Is it being continually fed by dynamic corporate worship? Do worshipers continually meet their majestic Lord and sense a deepening spiritual longing? Do you see members growing in their personal spiritual life? Is the church's prayer life characterized by deep and thorough prayer for God's blessing on every facet of life and ministry? The answers to these questions will indicate areas for which action plan outlines should prayerfully be generated.

Consider your church's ministries. Does your church offer a balance of elements—worship, nurture, outreach, and mercy ministries? Did the data collected to help formulate a vision indicate a discrepancy between needs—in both the congregation and the community—and programs? Each area needing modification calls for an action plan outline.

Consider your church's authority infrastructure. Does it conform to the biblically healthy pattern of accountable shepherd leadership that encourages the spiritual initiative of the flock? If the answer to this question is no, and the parties involved have demonstrated an unwillingness to change, it is highly likely that your church has not been able to get even this far in the process of preparing a vision statement and an action plan! Suppose you have elders who are unwilling to surrender power, as they perceive it, and unwilling to trust members' gifts. Suppose the elders cannot seem to exercise proper authority because of a family or clan that calls the shots. Suppose the pastor refuses to modify his own vision. In any of these scenarios, your church has a health problem that probably will have stopped the vision formulation process, for it will have prevented the kind of openness to self-evaluation and to spiritual change and growth that this process requires.

Once again we see that the things I have been recommending in this book stand or fall together! If they are to stand, the elders must be willing to lead as shepherds, maintaining accountability to God while nurturing the growth and initiative of Spirit-gifted members.

It may be that both the leadership and the laity have demonstrated the openness and humility necessary to bring them this far in the vision process, and that the process does suggest that the church's authority infrastructure needs revision. It may suggest, for example, that elders need to function more like shepherds, or that some mechanism must be devised, such as ministry centers, to engage the spiritual gifts of members. It may suggest that the pastor and the session need to work out some difficulties between them. It may suggest that some members exercising undue and illicit authority be disciplined. As you can easily see, such matters must be tended to by the session itself. It would be inappropriate for an action plan outline regarding such matters to be written by a committee outside the session! But if you have gotten this far in the process, chances are you have a session that has already demonstrated willingness to submit to the Lord's loving discipline, and which has already recognized the need for it.

Once the vision task force (or whoever) has identified key areas for modification, it makes a formal recommendation to the session that these areas be addressed. With this they complete their task.

Outlining concrete plans. Next, the session responds to this recommendation. For every area of potential modification, the session should appoint a small, four- or five-member committee. No elder or staff member need be on this committee. It is wise to include a member or two who ultimately will be involved in the proposed ministry. But a broad representation from the congregation provides a variety of perspectives and a complementarity of gifts that will strengthen the eventual proposal.

Each committee will study the need to which they've been assigned, and they will compose an action plan outline that addresses it.

Action plan outlines have the following key components:

- a specific objective—what is to be accomplished. Specificity—concreteness—is essential at this point. For example, don't say, "We need to pray more." Instead, say, "We want to start a program that will involve the whole congregation in methodically bringing before God every aspect of our church's life and ministry." Don't say, "We need to extend our Christian education opportunities to the community." Instead, say, "We want to start a radio program."

- a broad outline of how this will be accomplished. This may include, for example, remodeling a wing of the building, hiring a new staff person, or enlisting volunteers.
- estimates of when the ministry will begin, its duration, the manpower required by the ministry, the facilities required by the ministry, and what the ministry will cost.

You can see a sample of an action plan outline in appendix B.

It should take three to five months for all these outlines to be completed. Once a study committee completes its outline, it then submits it to the session. The study committee's task is completed.

Assembling the action plan. Once the outlines are viewed together, no doubt some adjustments will be necessary! Perhaps the total bill is outrageous. Perhaps all the plans, taken together, call for an unrealistic number of man-hours, given the size of the congregation and the level of commitment. Perhaps one change is more urgent or strategic than another. Obviously, we'll have to balance competing goods, massaging and prioritizing, so that the end result is a coherent whole that is achievable without internal conflict. Some action plan outlines will have to be scrapped, and others will have to be revised, in order to accommodate these considerations.

This is properly the session's task, for it involves spiritual oversight, assessing spiritual needs and opportunities, and directing responses, for which God holds elders accountable. Difficult choices are often involved, which have far-reaching implications for the congregation and the community.

Once the overarching action plan has been assembled, you will be able to compile several syntheses. You will be able to graph the expected total financial demands along a time line, showing how much money you will need by what time in order for you to carry out your plan. You will be able to do the same thing for your total manpower needs over time. You will be able to generate an estimate of anticipated growth, both in the number of members and in the amount of giving. You should also compile a time line that shows when new programs and activities will be phased in, and when relevant preparations will need to be completed. All of this information, synthetically compiled as it is, will guide your church's efforts, so that goals can be met smoothly. It will give you the kind of concrete mile markers that motivate everyone to keep on moving ahead.

The session formally adopts this action plan. This signals their commitment to communicate it, to espouse it, and to encourage and aid the flock in its realization.

The entire action plan can be published, dispersed, and discussed widely. It constitutes the concrete outworking of your church's fresh vision.

Implementing the action plan. All that remains is to push the start button! The session turns over the various action plan outlines to the appropriate ministry centers. Starting a Sunday school class on parenting? That goes to the Christian Education Ministry Center. Hiring a worship leader? The Worship Ministry Center will look into that. Developing a food distribution center? The deacons will carry that out.

At this point, you have everything you need in place to

move forward as a church. You don't just have a vague idea, but you know very clearly what to do, in what order, and by when. You also have in place everything you need to monitor that progress, to insure that you all stay on track, and to assess whether your plans are having their intended result. You will be able to recognize when a person or a group needs extra encouragement to continue in their efforts or help to solve a problem. You will be able to take note of plans that are working less efficiently than anticipated; you can collect ideas for your next revision! And in the process of writing your vision and your plan, you will have engaged and inspired members in this grand pursuit.

Leaders must continue to speak and function in terms of the church's vision! If we allow ourselves to forget it, we will lose the sense that we are doing what we do for a purpose. We will lose sight of the forest and get lost among the trees. Leaders, plan to encourage the troops continually. One way to do this is to help them see the progress you're making toward a goal. One way is to help them see, again and again, how what they're doing actualizes the church's divine purpose and mission.

Notice the session's involvement in this entire process. They don't do everything! In fact, their contribution, quantitatively speaking, is minor. Leadership is decentralized, and everybody gets into the act. But the session's involvement is strategic, so that the elders retain their God-given accountability. Thus, this vision-to-action process honors both biblical directives.

Health on the Rise

The overall procedure, from vision to plan to action, should significantly boost or insure your church's health! If your church's life and ministry express clear support for your chosen vision, your church is exhibiting good health. If, in the process of stating and implementing a vision, your church has also taken steps to reconstrue the elders' work as a ministry of shepherding, to exploit vibrant worship to motivate change, to use the Bible systematically in all activities and ministries, and to cultivate faith, then the vision process will be promoting health on many fronts simultaneously. You will know the joy of comprehending and capitalizing upon your church's God-ordained contribution to the universal purpose and mission that unify and define the bride of Christ.

Questions for Discussion

1. What are some areas that your church needs to modify in order to improve its spiritual health, to stimulate its spiritual life, or to increase the effectiveness of its ministry?

2. Try your hand at writing an action plan outline that addresses one of these areas. Be sure to include a specific objective, strategies for accomplishing it, and estimates of time, manpower, and cost.

3. Is your church willing to take part in a vision-to-action process?

Part IV

Christ's Beautiful Bride

Chapter 11 The Bottom Line: Divine Grace for Trust and Obedience

> **Healthy Practice #6:** The church must prayerfully seek the grace of God to build commitment to biblical health.

In this chapter, my argument is simple. God in His Word commands this model of church health, promising His blessing on us if we are obedient. As with any divine commands, God not only issues the commands, but also supplies the faith to believe and the determination to obey. Thus, in this matter of church health, as in any other area of life and obedience, we must prayerfully and humbly lay hold of the grace that works both the faith and the obedience we need to follow through.

Laying hold of God's grace to trust and obey is a healthy practice; of this I have no doubt. I have "field experience" with many churches. I have seen churches that simply do not appropriate any of this message. Some think they can't do it; others refuse to change or grow. They simply lack the faith to step out and do something. "Where is your faith?" I wish to admonish them (and many times I do). "Don't you believe that God will enable you to obey Him?"

The churches that mature in health and effect lasting change are the ones that come to God in brokenness and humility and beg Him to produce the obedience of faith in them.

How to Obey the Covenanting God

What is required is the same dynamic of obedience that you know so well in your own personal life, whether the issue is putting no other gods before Him, loving your neighbor, resisting temptation, or keeping your promises. God redeems you; He issues His commands. God calls upon you to believe Him, to trust that His commands are meant for your good, and to strive to obey them. And just as you were utterly dependent on Him to redeem you in the first place, so you are now utterly dependent on His grace to make you want to follow His commands and to bless your efforts.

This is the message of God's grace for the entire Christian life. We are saved by grace, but we also live by grace. Too often we deserve the scolding that Paul gave the Galatian believers:

> You foolish Galatians! Who has bewitched you? Before your very eyes Jesus Christ was clearly portrayed as crucified. I would like to learn just one thing from you: Did you receive the Spirit by observing the law, or by believing what you heard? Are you so foolish? After beginning with the Spirit, are you now trying to attain your goal by human effort? (Gal. 3:1–3)

God's redemption is a gracious gift. But so are His commands: God binds Himself forever to honor our obedience to His words. We can count on it that He'll never capriciously change His way of working. This is what we mean when we speak of the covenant.

Jesus' sacrifice was a gracious gift. But so is the Holy Spirit, whom He gives us to make us "ready and willing henceforth to serve Him" (Heidelberg Catechism, Q. 1). He calls us to obey; He alone can change our hearts to follow through.

When I first realized this, it made the whole concept of God's covenant personal and alive for me. Everything in the covenant is based on and powered by grace: God's faithful commitment to us in the law, the sacrifice that atones for my law-breaking, and the power for me to keep His ways. We sinful people can't even generate the faith or determination to obey Him apart from His work in our lives! I saw that His grace not only saved me without my contributing any effort, but also enabled me to go on from there and live by faith. My faith is not energized by my grit and willpower; it is energized by the same grace that saved me. Titus 2:11–14 says that the grace of God brings salvation and that it also "teaches us to say 'No' to ungodliness and worldly passions, and to live self-controlled, upright and godly lives." In giving Himself for us, Jesus redeemed us, purified us, and made us "eager to do what is good." Never should we believe that on our own we can or will muster up godly desires or obedience, for this wrongly belittles the extent of God's provision for us and the greatness of His power and love. And, on the positive side, to recognize the role of God's grace in living by faith frees and energizes us to live joyfully and even more effectively than if we wrongly believed that we are saved by grace but live by works.

Now, does this mean that we sit back and wait to be "zapped" with some supernatural empowerment—that we let go and let God, as people sometimes say? No! "Work out your salvation with fear and trembling," says Paul, "for it is God who works in you to will and to act according to his good purpose" (Phil. 2:12–13). Are you hungry to know Him better?

Do you love what He loves? Do you want to change your will to match His? If you do, that is ample evidence that God is working in you "to will and to act according to his good purpose."

We're talking in this book about *corporate* obedience, the belief and obedience of the church as a whole. Corporate obedience is not simply the total obedience of all the individuals in it. Of course, corporate obedience requires the faith and the obedience of individual members, but in essence it is the mutual agreement of the individuals that the body as a whole must follow Christ in obedience. And the same dynamic of obedience applies on this corporate level: God establishes the church through redemption; He instructs us concerning the nature of a healthy church; He gives the desire corporately to trust His promises and follow Him in obedience.

God Calls Our Church to Healthy Practices

What I've described is the dynamic of obedience—that is, how God enables us to obey. Obviously, I believe that God wants us to obey the instructions that I have set forth in this book. That assumes, of course, that the model of church health presented in this book is indeed the command of God.

Such a claim may sound audacious. But I am not making any claim about myself or my efforts. I am claiming that what I have presented here has authority precisely because it is what God Himself has commanded. As you have read this book, I trust that you have weighed my words against Scripture. You have already assessed whether my claims are supported by the Bible.

Does God intend that we keep the Bible as the hallmark of every church endeavor? Does He intend our worship, in which we meet Him, glimpse His awesome power, and experience afresh His sovereign love, to motivate us for ministry?

Does the Bible command the church to be the presence of Christ on earth, to fulfill the Great Commission? This implies that we must figure out how to do this in our local circumstance, utilizing our God-given resources. Taking steps to specify a vision and implement plans that fulfill it, while not directly commanded by Scripture, do actualize God's commands.

Does the Bible command us both to utilize individual members' Spirit-given gifts and to maintain accountable leadership? Does the Bible command our elders to be shepherds? Do these commands not imply that we must find a mechanism that allows us to balance them in a complementary way? Ministry centers, while not directly commanded by Scripture, form just such a mechanism.

Thus, God has explicitly commanded much of what this book enjoins. The remainder consists of strategies I have devised to implement those commands. The strategies do not carry a divine imprimatur; no doubt we'll all think of refinements that will make them more effective. But obedience to what God has commanded entails practical strategies like those described here. My experience indicates that the particular mechanisms recommended here, while conforming to Scripture, are effective in bringing greater health to a church.

Thus, I commend this concept of church health to you as one that is biblically enjoined. It is therefore something that we are corporately to obey. It is not optional! We cannot, with impunity, take it to be a matter of preference, decide that it does not fit our church, and ignore it. We reject God's Word at our peril. Obedience is the only legitimate response to the commands of the living God.

Our dear, covenanting God promises to deal with churches in light of His own specifications. He never changes the rules of the game, so to speak. He promises His blessing on our obedience—we can count on it. Not that our goal is the blessing; we always focus on the obedience. But we can always trust that obedience brings blessing. A healthy church will grow—naturally. God promises to equip us with the power to believe and to obey: "His divine power has given us everything we need for life and godliness. . . . For this very reason, make every effort to [obey God]. . . . For if you possess these qualities in increasing measure, they will keep you from being ineffective and unproductive in your knowledge of our Lord Jesus Christ" (2 Peter 1:3–8).

Prayerfully Lay Hold of God's Promises

If you grant that pursuing these healthy practices is divinely commanded, and that obeying any command involves looking to God also to put faith and obedience in our hearts, then it is clear what our church must do.

We must get on our knees *en masse*. We must pray for God graciously to work faith and obedience in our hearts. A great way to begin praying is to use the desperate words of the father of the demon-stricken boy: in response to Jesus' query, he exclaimed, "I do believe; help me overcome my unbelief!" (Mark 9:24). We need God not only to work the miracle of obedience, but also to work the miracle of faith. We can't even change our own heart's desires.

In an earlier chapter, I recommended regular corporate prayer for your church. Here I return to that exhortation. It should be clear by now why this whole endeavor must be saturated with prayer.

Getting on our knees as a church calls for corporate soul-searching, for admission of guilt, for brokenness, for acknowledging our utter need of God's mercy and power. It may not be pleasant, humanly speaking. It may be agonizing.

But it may also spell the end of your agony, as you as a body do what you may have been resisting for years—submit to Christ, cast yourself on Him. It may be that you as a church have come to the end of the road. You may feel yourselves to be on the brink of death. You may feel yourselves to be "without hope, save in God's sovereign mercy." If this phrase from my denomination's new member's confession of faith describes how your church feels about itself, then count yourselves blessed already by the powerful working of the Spirit! He has broken you; now He can and will work.

What is more likely to be the case is that, while some members of your church are eager to move forward in obedience, others show no interest or even exercise active resistance. A step like this can bring to the surface what has been simmering for a long time underneath. Think of it: we've been talking about the shaping of lines of authority. This may challenge the power struggles that have swirled around your "king of the mountain." You're asking people to change, but some may feel that they've already arrived, spiritually speaking, and do not need to change.

If you belong to the group that wishes to follow Christ in matters of church health, then you must comport yourselves as He did. Peter calls us to avoid doing wrong; by doing good, we silence the ignorant talk of foolish men:

> But if you suffer for doing good and you endure it, this
> is commendable before God. To this you were called,
> because Christ suffered for you, leaving you an exam-

ple, that you should follow in his steps. "He committed no sin, and no deceit was found in his mouth." When they hurled their insults as him, he did not retaliate; when he suffered, he made no threats. Instead, he entrusted himself to him who judges justly. (1 Peter 2:20–23)

If anybody had a "right to retaliate," Jesus did! He wants us to endure perceived wrongs with the grace that can come only from entrusting ourselves to the one who judges justly.

This, too, drives us to our knees in prayer, for God alone changes hearts. Do not pray only that He will change your opponents' hearts! Pray that He will change yours.

If change toward health is to come in your church, the proponents of change must eventually include the elders. As I have said before, a lay movement that remains so is doomed. Yes, a move toward health may begin among unordained members, but then it must spread to the leadership. This calls for prayer, for much talk, for encouragement, and perhaps for respectful confrontation. Perhaps most effective of all is the enlistment of outside help. This sort of situation confirms my confidence in a presbyterian grouping of churches, in which individual pastors and elders are accountable to their colleagues in other churches. It is within this context that I serve as a church consultant. Many times God has used my ministry to afford a church an outside perspective.

If your church's ordained leaders embrace the need to grow in health, then God has through their shepherd leadership provided the means for the entire church's growth. We've talked about how elders function as movers and shakers, as agents of change, as leaders who inspire confidence through nurturing ministry. We've talked about the importance of setting an example and communicating. We've talked about the importance of shepherds treating the sheep's contributions with integrity. It may be, in your church, that true shepherd leadership will begin in this hour of soul-searching and crisis. If your elders have not been fulfilling their God-given calling, and now they have entered into this humble petition for God's grace, you can bet that their submission to Christ as leaders will be this process's first and most significant fruit.

Whether fledgling or seasoned, the elders' leadership will move the church body forward in obedience. In the event of open resistance, elders alone are divinely authorized to administer ecclesiastical discipline.

God's ordained instruments of change include the elders as they shepherd their flock. They include the Word of God, the living and powerful sword of the Spirit. They also include the experience of corporate worship, as we saw in an earlier chapter. Godly obedience never occurs in a vacuum. It always comes as the grateful response to God's prior, unconditioned love. Is your church's "obedience quotient" low? You should check your church's "Scripture quotient" and "worship quotient"! Each should present the holy God of the covenant, the gracious Savior of souls, the powerful Spirit who turns hearts of stone into hearts of flesh. You should expect that, in answer to your church's prayers, God will utilize one or more of these instruments.

The Word of God promises to work in and through those who cast themselves on Him, whether individually or corporately. He dwells with those of humble and contrite heart; He teaches those who fear Him; He draws near to those who draw near to Him. I can virtually guarantee that once your church, as a body, truly cries out to God, the river of God's grace will carry you forward into biblical health. God does not start that river flowing once He sees our earnest desire; our earnest desire itself results from that river of grace! To God alone be glory as the fountain of every good thing. He has already begun His work in you by causing your heart to long for Him.

Then act, in the strength that God provides. Step out in faith; act in obedience to His Word. Seek to implement the practices set forth in this book on the authority of Scripture. You do not need special leading before you get started! You simply need to obey. If a father tells a child to clean his room, no further special revelation is needed; it would be a mistake, perhaps a painful one, for the child to wait for further prompting! Be assured that every step you take, while it calls for great action on your part, also counts as evidence of God's working through you "to will and to act according to his good pleasure."

Christ's Beautiful Bride

I would have you share my love for Christ's bride. That more than anything has driven me to write this book. I love the church because I love Christ. I love it because it is Christ's presence on earth. My study of church health, the results of which I have communicated to you, intensifies my passion, just as getting to know a beloved person draws us to deeper love and further study. I see more clearly God's design for His church, what He intends to bring about in and through us. And I love it and Him for it.

I earnestly want you to have a similar response, for this passion is that spiritual longing that draws us to Christ. It will draw you onward in knowing and loving Him. It will draw your church together in unified pursuit of His richest blessing for those who seek Him. Loving Christ means loving His church and longing for it to grow in health to image Him and influence the world in His name.

Let your growing passion for Christ and for His beautiful bride drive your church to actualize His design for health, to be all that you can be.

> To him who is able to keep you from falling and to present you before his glorious presence without fault and with great joy—to the only God our Savior be glory, majesty, power and authority, through Jesus Christ our Lord, before all ages, now and forevermore! Amen. (Jude 24–25)

Questions for Discussion

1. Assess your church's current status with respect to the matters discussed in this chapter.
   a. Is it ready as a body to move forward in church health?
   b. Are some of the people anxious to move forward in church health, while others are not?
   c. Is the "opposition" passively ignorant or actively resistant?
   d. Are some or all of your elders among those who wish to move forward in church health?
2. What concrete steps do you need to take to encourage corporate trust and obedience in church health? Consider the following elements discussed in this chapter:
   • active soul-searching; repentant prayer for God's grace

- elders ready to lead as shepherds
- healthy lines and levels of communication
- vibrant worship
- the authoritative preaching of God's vision for His church
- problems preventing the church from moving forward in faith
- the need for, and availability of, outside counsel

Appendices

Appendix A Ministry Center Guidelines

For each ministry center, the session must develop a set of guidelines that specifically describe or stipulate the following items:

Guidelines that will read the same for every center:

- the church's vision statement
- the organizational arrangement by which elders exercise oversight and members exercise initiative in ministry
- the procedures that the center should follow when seeking permission to use facilities, cars, etc., in extraordinary circumstances
- financial policies a center must observe, and a procedure to follow should the center find that it must exceed its budget
- procedures to follow in order to integrate this center's concepts into those of other ministry centers
- an annual deadline for the center to draft and submit for the session's approval its measurable objectives and its proposed mechanism for self-evaluation

○

Guidelines that will be unique for each center:

- the ministry center's specific purpose
- any unique application of the church's doctrinal position and/or its vision statement, which the session expects that ministry center to accomplish: I say "unique" to insure against the common temptation for elders to flesh out the guidelines on the level intended to be drawn up by the centers themselves. That would undermine the purpose of the guidelines and weaken their impact.
- the extent of the center's supervisory responsibility to maintain the facilities, cars, etc., that it uses
- the center's budget allotment
- any unique organizational relationship between this ministry center and other centers: Special attention must be given to the working relationship between elders and deacons.

Guidelines must be constructed in such a way that ministry center members can exercise their spiritual gifts, talents, creativity, and ingenuity to enhance the vision statement's impact on the church, to accomplish the center's specific purpose, and to do so comfortably within these stipulated parameters.

Guidelines normally consist of general statements that do not include specific dates, details, or methods. They should be clear and easily understood.

Some guidelines may have appended to them an amplifying statement which uniquely specifies a center's application of the guidelines or gives instructions for planning. For example, the Christian Education Ministry Center may be instructed to orient all candidates for membership with regard to the church's vision statement, or to offer regular adult Sunday school classes on the Catechism. Note that neither the guideline nor the appended instruction incorporates details for accomplishing this goal.

Guidelines should be drafted by a task force consisting of a few members of the church, including people with specific experience and expertise in that area of ministry. Proposed guidelines will be submitted to the session. After a short period of clarification and negotiation, the session will approve (or disapprove) these guidelines.

Guidelines should be implemented with a view to their spirit, rather than their letter. No human code can possibly cover every contingency. When unprecedented situations arise without warning, ministry centers can exercise some freedom of interpretation, making a note where necessary to clarify matters when that guideline is reviewed.

Guidelines must be reviewed and revised on an annual basis, so that the church remains free to grow and adapt according to the Holy Spirit's leading and provision.

Appendix B A Sample Action Plan Outline

CATEGORY: LIFE
ACTION PLAN OUTLINE #1.1
Church Ministry Display Chart
Prayer Ministry

SPECIFIC OBJECTIVE: The congregation should undergird the entire life, ministry, and leadership personnel with prayer on a daily basis. This should include up-to-date data about activities in this church.

STRATEGIES/IDEAS: A task force should develop a comprehensive *church ministry display chart* (CMDC). The outline to be used is the list of the functions of the church, plus facilities, finances, staff and their families, and unusual needs.

For each line on the outline, pray for the program(s) involved and the key personnel responsible.

The task force should develop a plan to enroll volunteers to pray through the CMDC within three weeks and then start over.

A prayer coordinator should be appointed. He or she would:

- seek volunteers on an ongoing basis, with the goal being close to 100 percent participation by the members of the congregation;

- encourage the volunteers to persevere;
- keep the basic data updated;
- occasionally relay human-interest anecdotes and/or needs;
- share some reactions from the volunteers with the congregation.

ASSUMPTIONS:
- Time frame: appoint the task force immediately, to report to the session in three weeks. Implement the CMDC program directly thereafter.
- Budget: none, except for some copying and stapling.
- Manpower: prayer coordinator.

The following graphic will serve as a basic model for constructing a CMDC. It is not intended to be complete.

FUNCTION	PROGRAM	PERSON
WORSHIP:		
Services	8:15 a.m.	
	11:00 a.m.	
	Evening	
	Easter sunrise	
	Christmas	
	Etc.	
Prayer Life	Midweek service	
	Cell group	
	Etc.	
NURTURE:		
Instruction	S.S. superintendent	
	S.S. teachers	

	Orientation classes
	Officer training
	Teacher training
	Community Bible classes
	Cell groups
	Etc.
Fellowship	——
Discipling	——
Discipline	——
Sacraments	——
Shepherding	——

MERCY:

Diaconal (church family)	——
Regional (beyond church family)	——
Worldwide	——

OUTREACH:

Evangelism	——
Missions (national, international, educational, etc.)	——
"Saltiness"	——

FACILITY NEEDS: ——

FINANCIAL NEEDS: ——

STAFF AND FAMILIES: ——

UNUSUAL NEEDS: ——

Notes

Chapter 3: The Bible: The Hallmark of a Healthy Church

1. Mike Regele, *Death of the Church* (Grand Rapids: Zondervan, 1995), 72.

Chapter 4: Divine Motivation for Spiritual Life and Ministry

1. C. S. Lewis, *The Last Battle* (New York: MacMillan, 1956), chap. 15.
2. Edmund P. Clowney, *Living in Christ* (Philadelphia: Great Commission Publications, 1982), 12–13.
3. Augustine, *Confessions* 1.1 (trans. John K. Ryan [New York: Doubleday, 1960]).

Chapter 7: The Elder's Official Responsibilities

1. Donald J. MacNair, *Restoration—God's Way* (Philadelphia: Great Commission Publications, 1987), chap. 2.

Chapter 9: Your Vision: Uniquely You

1. See, for example, George Barna, *The Power of Vision: How You Can Capture and Apply God's Vision for Your Ministry* (Ventura, Calif.: Regal, 1992), 15.